# Plan to Succeed With Your LifeWealth

Helping Dreams Become Reality

Hilgardt Lamprecht| The LifeWealth Group

Copyright © 2023 by Hilgardt Lamprecht.

All rights reserved. No part of this publication may be reproduced, distributed, or transmitted in any form or by any means, including photocopying, recording, or other electronic or mechanical methods, without the prior written permission of the publisher, except in the case of brief quotations embodied in critical reviews and certain other noncommercial uses permitted by copyright law. For permission requests, write to the publisher at the address below. These materials are provided to you by Hilgardt Lamprecht for informational purposes only and Hilgardt Lamprecht and Advisors Excel, LLC expressly disclaim any and all liability arising out of or relating to your use of same. The provision of these materials does not constitute legal or investment advice and does not establish an attorney-client relationship between you and Hilgardt Lamprecht. No tax advice is contained in these materials. You are solely responsible for ensuring the accuracy and completeness of all materials as well as the compliance, validity, and enforceability of all materials under any applicable law. The advice and strategies found within may not be suitable for every situation. You are expressly advised to consult with a qualified attorney or other professional in making any such determination and to determine your legal or financial needs. No warranty of any kind, implied, expressed, or statutory, including but not limited to the warranties of title and non-infringement of third-party rights, is given with respect to this publication.

Hilgardt Lamprecht/The LifeWealth Group
270 W Plant St. Suite 240 Winter Garden FL 34787
www.thelifewealthgroup.com

Book layout ©2023 Advisors Excel, LLC

Plan to Succeed With Your LifeWealth/Hilgardt Lamprecht.

ISBN 9798852199997

Hilgardt Lamprecht is registered as an Investment Adviser Representative and is a licensed insurance agent in the states of FL, AL, AZ, CA, DC, GA, IL, MA, MD, MI, MN, MO, MS, MT, NC, NH, NV, OH, SC, SD, TX, VA, and WI. His state insurance license numbers are OE56515 in California and 1237880 in Texas.

Securities offered only by duly registered individuals through Madison Avenue Securities, LLC (MAS), member FINRA/SIPC. Insurance products are offered through the insurance business The LifeWealth Group. The LifeWealth Group is also an Investment Advisory practice that offers products and services through AE Wealth Management, LLC (AEWM), a Registered Investment Advisor. AEWM does not offer insurance products. The insurance products offered by The LifeWealth Group are not subject to Investment Advisor requirements. MAS and The LifeWealth Group are not affiliated companies.The contents of this book are provided for informational purposes only and are not intended to serve as the basis for any financial decisions. Any tax, legal, or estate planning information is general in nature. It should not be construed as legal or tax advice. Always consult an attorney or tax professional regarding the applicability of this information to your unique situation.Please remember that converting an employer plan account to a Roth IRA is a taxable event. Increased taxable income from the Roth IRA conversion may have several consequences. Be sure to consult with a qualified tax advisor before making any decisions regarding your IRA.

Information presented is believed to be factual and up-to-date, but we do not guarantee its accuracy, and it should not be regarded as a complete analysis of subjects discussed. All expressions of opinion are those of the author as of the date of publication and are subject to change. Content should not be construed as personalized investment advice nor should it be interpreted as an offer to buy or sell any securities mentioned. A financial advisor should be consulted before implementing any strategies presented.

Investing involves risk, including the potential loss of principal. No investment strategy can guarantee a profit or protect against loss in periods of declining values. Any references to protection benefits or guaranteed/lifetime income streams refer only to fixed insurance products, not securities or investment products. Insurance and annuity product guarantees are backed by the financial strength and claims-paying ability of the issuing insurance company. The LifeWealth Group is not affiliated with the U.S. government or any governmental agency. AE Wealth Management provides services without regard to religious affiliation and the views of individual advisors are not necessarily the views of AE Wealth Management.

CFP Board owns the certification marks CFP®, CERTIFIED FINANCIAL PLANNER™, and CFP® in the U.S.

*Any names used in the examples in this book are hypothetical only and do not represent actual clients.6/23-1797586*

*"The poorest of all people is not the person without a dollar, but a person without a dream."*

*~ Catherine DeVrye*

I dedicate this book to my teachers and mentors who invested in me and deposited wisdom.

I also dedicate this book to my three boys, Hilton, Chris, and Liam. I am very proud of all three of you.

And I thank my bride, Janice, who has lived these stories and principles, which we both thank God for giving us. Implementing His principles leads to a life of freedom.

# Table of Contents

The Importance of Planning ............................................. I
Longevity ................................................................... 1
Taxes ...................................................................... 21
Market Volatility ....................................................... 27
Retirement Income .................................................... 37
Social Security ......................................................... 55
401(k)s & IRAs ........................................................ 71
Annuities ................................................................ 85
Estate & Legacy ....................................................... 93
Women Retire Too ................................................... 103
Charity .................................................................. 117
Finding a Financial Professional ................................. 125
Acknowledgments ................................................... 131
*About the Author* .................................................. 133

PREFACE: HILGARDT LAMPRECHT
# The Importance of Planning

The phone rang, and I could tell my mother was crying. Immediately I assumed the worst.

"What's wrong, Mom? Did Dad die?" Fortunately, Dad was fine. Instead, Mom's despair centered on me. My final accounting exam results had arrived in the mail, and Mom reported the findings. My score fell into the lower half of the class. I failed.

Essentially, the grade nullified my work for the entire academic year I spent as a fourth-year student aspiring to become a Chartered accountant (South African for CPA). Driving to that exam, I understood its importance. It was the big kahuna, I told myself. The drive, along one of the national roads within my native South Africa, took me to the beautiful mountain town of Stellenbosch.

The familiar scenery, however, had not relieved my stress. The year had been my toughest, academically. For ten months, I struggled through exams lasting from three to five hours each. I spent two more months preparing for the final exam. Yet, I was still unsure of myself. Did I possess the knowledge to pass the last hurdle?

Another equally powerful and unsettling thought: Did I really want to be an accountant?

Despite my uncertainties, I carried on and rode out the exam. The next day, I boarded my second plane ride ever. I visited my girlfriend, also a South African, who lived in America. She lived and worked in America because it was common for young South African college graduates to work overseas to earn foreign currency that could expedite the payoff of student loans.

After about two and a half months, I made the decision of a lifetime. I proposed on one knee in Clearwater Beach. I didn't have a ring, but I explained that my mother could hook us up with a good one because she was in the jewelry business. Janice accepted, then we returned to her apartment and called her family so I could ask permission from her parents.

We couldn't be happier, especially since I had landed a job with Ernst and Young, one of the top five accounting firms in the world. Our future aligned perfectly. After all, I was becoming a chartered accountant. A great future awaited us.

It was then that my mom called, sobbing uncontrollably before breaking the devastating news, "Son, you failed." What do you do with that information now that it has shattered a promising future?

Humbled, I moved back in with my parents, tacked another year of student loans into my education, reenrolled, and began studying again for my CPA. Yet my lack of desire to become an accountant weighed on my mind. So did my wedding and all the planning that goes into that. Janice remained steadfast and encouraged me to forge ahead, though my desperation demanded additional guidance.

I did the only thing that made sense to me. I prayed to God to reveal my future. For three months, I repeatedly prayed, asking God what he wanted me to do with my academic background. As he revealed himself, he told me to go to America—the land of the dreamers, the doers, and the givers. I could blend my business, tax planning, and accounting skills to help Americans realize their financial dreams and retirement vision.

With a plan in place, my renewed enthusiasm inspired me to complete my fifth academic year. I knew my Bachelor of Accountancy degree would not lead to preparing annual returns chronicling taxpayers' finances. Instead, I would apply my education to help plan clients' financial futures.

Two days after my final accounting exam, Janice and I married. Four months later, we again boarded a plane for Florida. We arrived with two suitcases and the beautiful money notes symbolic of my homeland. South African bills feature pictures of lions, tigers, elephants, and rhinos. I exchanged those notes for bills with images of iconic American leaders I didn't recognize.

For that matter, I didn't know how far $1, $10, or $100 could stretch in terms of the groceries I would purchase or the utilities I would pay.

Most people have these same questions when they view their finances. They ask if their money will last their lifetimes and potentially even allow them to leave some to their loved ones.

Looking back at our first days building a life together in a foreign land, Janice and I constructed a modest spending plan. We started by simply writing down what we spent and how much our purchases cost. We gradually gained more courage and motivation to learn more about finances and, soon, we gained confidence knowing we understood the power of planning.

A quarter-century later, our family of experienced financial professionals at The LifeWealth Group works with more than 400 families, helping them see their dreams come true. We have multiple advisors in our firm and we have all seen countlessly how everything significant starts with a dream.

Based on experiences that led me to found and grow The LifeWealth Group, my personal philosophy is that the poorest of all men is not the man without a dollar, but it's the man without a dream. Everything significant in life starts with a dream.

# Potential Risks to Your Ideal Retirement

Ever feel like life gets in the way and prevents you from doing things you should not ignore? I think if we're honest with ourselves, we've all put off obligations we know are important.

In your case, you may be reading this book because it's time to get serious about financial planning and, specifically, devising a way to best prepare for retirement. A retirement plan should be based on more components than just your investments or your finances. The preparation of that strategy begins with your desires, ambitions, and goals for this fulfilling season of life.

There's no such thing as a silly question. Not when one of the most common questions we hear from people regarding retirement is, "Am I going to be okay?" Often, it seems, people are reluctant to meet with financial professionals because they worry they might sound uneducated. Yet, it's understandable for you to be a novice when it comes to financial issues and retirement concerns. You've been busy with your lives and your careers. Time spent away from work has meant time spent being around those you love and engaging in the activities you enjoy. Retirement provides the opportunity to do even more of that, while not fretting over work obligations.

Concerns people have about what they may encounter during retirement can be far-reaching and still perfectly legitimate. For a quick snapshot, I want to provide a brief sampling of wide-ranging issues that can come up during discussions about what to potentially brace for in retirement. This book will touch on many of these issues in further detail.

**Politics:** A presidential election often stirs emotions regarding potential effects on the economy. Investors grow anxious about how a new president can influence market returns. It's Congress, however, that establishes tax laws and passes spending bills. Yet the president can indirectly affect the economy and the stock market in various ways such as the appointment of policymakers, development of international relations, and influential sway on new legislation.

**Taxes:** An example of a president's influence can be cited in signature legislation passed during Donald Trump's presidency, the Tax Cuts and Jobs Act of 2017. However, our tax system remains progressive, so the more you earn, the higher the tax rate within each tax bracket of subsequently higher income. A thorough understanding of tax regulations can be crucial. A financial professional can help identify potential issues a tax professional can help solve.

**Inflation:** Government spending, which most recently spiked with relief packages designed to assist U.S. citizens during the COVID-19 pandemic, can fuel concerns of inflationary hikes stemming from an influx of money thrust at the same consumer goods. A retiree's income can be impacted by the effect inflation can have on a fixed budget. The value of currency decreases because inflation erodes purchasing power.

**Health pandemic:** The coronavirus outbreak could impact how Americans view risks and re-examine healthy habits. That, potentially, could be one of the effects of COVID-19 as we assess how long a pandemic can last and if others will occur in our lifetimes. The cost of health care can be surprising throughout retirement. It could become an issue people focus on even more following the pandemic, which had a particularly acute impact on some U.S. elder care facilities.

**Cybersecurity:** Think you'll give up your smartphone in retirement? No way, right? It's here to stay, along with other intellectual gadgetry, including devices that have not been patented or invented. Retirees are becoming more tech-savvy, yet they can also be more trusting, which can be problematic when responding to potential scammers by phone, text, or email. Cybercrime often uses technology to target potential victims. Scammers, much like technology, figure to only grow more sophisticated over time.

CHAPTER 1

# Longevity

You would think the prospect of the grave would loom more frightening as we age, yet many retirees say their number one concern is actually running out of money in their twilight years.[1] This concern is, unfortunately, justified, in part, because of one significant factor: We're living longer.

According to the Social Security Administration's 2011 Trustee Report, in 1950, the average life expectancy for a sixty-five-year-old man was seventy-eight, and the average for a sixty-five-year-old woman was eighty-one. In the 2023 Trustees Report issued by the SSA, those averages were 81.94 and 84.66, respectively.[2]

The bottom line of many retirees' budget woes comes down to this: They just didn't plan to live so long. Now, when we are younger and in our working years, that's not something we necessarily see as a bad thing; don't some people fantasize about living forever or, at least, reaching the ripe old age of one hundred?

However, with a longer lifespan, as we near retirement, we face a few snags. Our resources are finite—we only have so much money to provide income—but our lifespans can be

---

[1] Liz Weston. nerdwallet.com. March 25, 2021. "Will You Really Run Out of Money in Retirement?" https://www.nerdwallet.com/article/finance/will-you-really-run-out-of-money-in-retirement
[2] Social Security Administration. 2023 Trustees Report. "Actuarial Life Table" https://www.ssa.gov/oact/STATS/table4c6.html

unpredictably long, perhaps longer than our resources allow. Also, longer lives don't necessarily equate with healthier lives. The longer you live, the more money you will likely need to spend on health care, even excluding long-term care needs like nursing homes.

You will also run into inflation. If you don't plan to live another twenty-five years but end up doing so, inflation at an average 3 percent will approximately double the price of goods over that time period. Put a harsh twist on that and the buying power of a ninety-year-old will be half of what they possessed if they retired at sixty-five.[3]

Because we don't necessarily get to have our cake and eat it, too, our collective increased longevity hasn't necessarily increased the healthy years of our lives. Typically, our life-extending care most widely applies to the time in our lives where we will need more care in general. Think of common situations like a pacemaker at eighty-five, or cancer treatment at seventy-eight.

"Wow, Hilgardt," I can hear you say. "Way to start with the good news first."

I know, I've painted a grim picture, but all I'm concerned about here is cost. It's hard to put a dollar sign on life, but that is essentially what we're talking about when discussing longevity and finances. Living longer isn't a bad thing; it just costs more, and one key to a sound retirement strategy is preparing for it in advance.

Freedom in retirement is more likely when we plan for the "what ifs" of life *and* when we are more excited about what we are retiring to rather than retiring from. For example, a potential client—we'll call him Ray—comes to see me with concerns about retiring.

Ray is a business owner ready to step away from the pressures of being a CEO, but he wants to be sure his wife's

---

[3] Bob Sullivan, Benjamin Curry. Forbes. April 28, 2021. "Inflation And Retirement Investments: What You Need to Know."
https://www.forbes.com/advisor/retirement/inflation-retirement-investments/

financial future is secure if he passes away first. He also is passionate about supporting several local non-profits, even in retirement.

Like most business owners, the proceeds from the sale of Ray's company would make up the majority of the capital he'll need for retirement, so he may want to plan to categorize the proceeds into three buckets. The first bucket of capital could be the money he and his wife need to help protect their retirement to plan for life's "what ifs." The second bucket could be dedicated to charitable giving so Ray and his wife can live out their desire to impact their community positively. The last bucket may be money he can reinvest in whatever opportunities feed his entrepreneurial spirit going forward.

With a thoughtful approach like this, Ray and his wife, we'll call her Mary, could have the potential freedom in retirement to pour their lives into those areas that give them the most satisfaction. And when either one of them passes away, the surviving spouse should be positioned to live with confidence that he or she has enough money for the rest of their life, even if they run into unexpected circumstances or they live longer than expected.

I believe the combination of *life* and *financial* planning can offer clients with the potential for a newfound energy and freedom to confidently transition to retirement.

## Retiring Early

A key part of planning for retirement revolves around retirement income. After all, retirement is cutting the cord that tethers you to your employer—and your monthly check. However, that check often comes with many other benefits, particularly health care. Health care is often the thing that can unexpectedly put dreams for an early retirement on hold. Some employers offer health benefits to their retired workers, but that number has declined drastically over the past several decades. In 1988, among employers who offered health benefits to their workers, 66 percent offered health benefits to their retirees. In 2022, that number was 21 percent.[4]

So, with employer-offered retirement health benefits on the wane, this becomes a major point of concern for anyone who is looking to retire, particularly those who are looking to retire before age sixty-five, when they would become eligible for Medicare coverage. Fidelity estimates that the average retired couple at age sixty-five will need approximately $315,000 for health care expenses in retirement, not including long-term care.[5] Do you think it's likely that cost will decrease?

Even if you are working until age sixty-five or have plans to cover your health expenses until that point, I often have clients who incorrectly assume Medicare is their golden ticket to cover all expenses. That is simply not the case.

# Retiring Later

Planning for a long life in retirement partly depends on when you retire. While many people end up retiring earlier than they anticipated—due to injuries, layoffs, family crises, and other unforeseen circumstances—continuing to work past age sixty (and even sixty-five) is still a viable option for others and can be an excellent way to help establish financial comfort in retirement.

There are many reasons for this. For one, you obviously still earn a paycheck and the benefits accompanying it. Medical coverage and beefing up your retirement accounts with further savings can be significant by themselves but continuing your income also should keep you from dipping into your retirement funds, further allowing them the opportunity to grow.

---

[4] Henry J. Kaiser Family Foundation. October 27, 2022. "2022 Employer Health Benefits Survey Section Eleven: Retiree Health Benefits." https://www.kff.org/report-section/ehbs-2022-section-11-retiree-health-benefits/

[5] Fidelity Viewpoints. Fidelity. May 6, 2021. "How to Plan for Rising Health Care Costs." https://www.fidelity.com/viewpoints/personal-finance/plan-for-rising-health-care-costs

Additionally, for many workers, their nine-to-five job is more than just clocking in and out. Having a sense of purpose can keep us active physically, mentally, and socially. That kind of activity and level of engagement may also help stave off many of the health problems that plague retirees. Avoiding a sedentary life is one of the advantages of staying plugged into the workforce, if possible.

Just after the sale of his company, another client of ours—let's call him Andrew—was introduced to me by his CPA. I could tell that Andrew was lost because he was astonished to find out how little money he had left after paying taxes and transaction costs on the sale. He told me angrily that if the CPA had told him how little money he would have left afterward, he would never have sold his company.

I continued to work with Andrew for the next two years, taking the money he did receive from the sale of the company and helping him invest it in his future. Looking back over those two years, he was more dissatisfied with the fact that he decided to sell his company than he was with the money that came from it.

The piece that seemed to be eating at him was the fact that he wasn't clear about what he would do with the rest of his life. He was in his mid-fifties and felt lost and purposeless. Like many business owners and successful entrepreneurs that dream of early retirement, he retired without figuring out what's next. He didn't take the time to understand what he was retiring to but was more focused on what he was retiring from.

Over my career, I have found this to be one of the crucial conversations to help people think through that transition in the best way possible. Retirement becomes exponentially more fulfilling and exciting when you understand what you are retiring to.

# Health Care

Take a second to reflect on your health care plan. Although working up to or even past age sixty-five would allow you to avoid a coverage gap between your working years and Medicare, that may not be an option for you. Even if it is, when you retire, you will need to make some decisions about what kind of insurance coverage you may need to supplement your Medicare. Are there any medical needs you have that may require coverage in addition to Medicare? Did your parents or grandparents have any inherited medical conditions you might consider using a special savings plan to cover?

These are all questions that are important to review with your financial professional so you can be sure you have enough money put aside for health care.

# Long-Term Care

Longevity means the need for long-term care is statistically more likely to happen. If you intend to pass on a legacy, planning for long-term care is paramount, since most estimates project nearly 70 percent of Americans will need some type of it.[6] However, this may be one of the biggest, most stressful pieces of longevity planning I encounter in my work. For one thing, who wants to talk about the point in their lives when they may feel the most limited? Who wants to dwell on what will happen if they no longer can toilet, bathe, dress, or feed themselves?

I get it; this is a less-than-fun part of planning. But a little bit of preparation now can go a long way!

When it comes to your longevity, just like with your goals, one of the important things to do is sit and dream. It may not be the fun, road-trip-to-the-Grand-Canyon kind of dreaming,

---

[6] LongTermCare.gov. February 18, 2020. "How Much Care Will You Need?" https://acl.gov/ltc/basic-needs/how-much-care-will-you-need

but you can spend time envisioning how you want your twilight years to look.

For instance, if it is important for you to live in your home for as long as possible, who will provide for the day-to-day fixes and to-dos of housework if you become ill? Will you set aside money for a service, or do you have relatives or friends nearby whom you could comfortably allow to help you? Do you prefer in-home care over a nursing home or assisted living? This could be a good time to discuss the possibility of moving into a retirement community versus staying where you are or whether it's worth moving to another state and leaving relatives behind.

These are all important factors to discuss with your spouse and children, as *now* is the right time to address questions and concerns. For instance, is aging in place more important to one spouse than the other? Are the friends or relatives who live nearby emotionally, physically, and financially capable of helping you for a time if you face an illness?

Many families I meet with find these conversations very uncomfortable, particularly when children discuss nursing home care with their parents. A knee-jerk reaction for many is to promise they will care for their aging parents. This is noble and well-intentioned, but there needs to be an element of realism here. Does "help" from an adult child mean they stop by and help you with laundry, cooking, home maintenance, and bills? Or does it mean they move you into their spare room when you have hip surgery? Are they prepared to help you use the restroom and bathe if that becomes difficult for you to do on your own?

I don't mean to discourage families from caring for their own; this can be a profoundly admirable relationship when it works out. However, I've seen families put off planning for late-in-life care based on a tenuous promise that the adult children would care for their parents, only to watch as the support system crumbles. Sometimes this is because the assumed caregiver hasn't given serious thought to the preparation they would need, both in a formal sense and regarding their personal physical, emotional, and financial commitments. This is often also because we can't see the future: Alzheimer's disease and other maladies of old age can exact a heavy toll. When a loved one reaches the point where he or she is at risk of wandering away or needs help with two or more activities of daily living, it can be more than one person or family can realistically handle.

If you know what you want, communicate with your family about both the best-case and worst-case scenarios. Then, hope for the best, and plan for the worst.

## Realistic Cost of Care

Wrapped up in your planning should be a consideration for the cost of long-term care. The potential costs for such care and treatment can be underestimated, especially by those who have maintained robust health and find it difficult to envision future declines to their condition.

Another piece of planning for long-term care costs is anticipating inflation. It's common knowledge that prices have been and keep rising, which can lower your purchasing power on everything from food to medical care. Long-term care is a big piece of the inflation-disparity pie.

While local costs vary from state to state, here's the national median for various forms of long-term care (plus projections that account for a 3 percent annual inflation, so you can see what I am referencing):[7]

---

[7] Genworth Financial. June 2022. "Cost of Care Survey 2022." https://www.genworth.com/aging-and-you/finances/cost-of-care.html

| Long-Term Care Costs: Inflation | | | | |
|---|---|---|---|---|
| | Home Health Care, Homemaker Services | Adult Day Care | Assisted Living | Nursing Home (semi-private room) |
| Annual 2021 | $59,488 | $20,280 | $54,000 | $94,900 |
| Annual 2031 | $79,947 | $27,255 | $72,571 | $127,538 |
| Annual 2041 | $107,442 | $36,628 | $97,530 | $171,400 |
| Annual 2051 | $144,393 | $49,225 | $131,072 | $230,347 |

# Fund Your Long-Term Care

One common mistakes I see are those who haven't planned for long-term care because they assume the government will provide everything. But that's a big misconception. The government has two health insurance programs: Medicare and Medicaid. These can greatly assist you in your health care needs in retirement but usually don't provide enough coverage to cover all your health care costs in retirement. My firm isn't a government outpost, so we don't get to make decisions when it comes to forming policy and specifics about either one of these programs. I'm going to give an overview of both, but if you want to dive into the details of these programs, you can visit www.Medicare.gov and www.Medicaid.gov.

### *Medicare*

Medicare covers those aged sixty-five and older and those who are disabled. Medicare's coverage of any nursing-home-related health issues is limited. It might cover your nursing home stay if it is not a "custodial" stay, and it isn't long-term. For example, if you break a bone or suffer a stroke, stay in a nursing home for rehabilitative care, and then return home, Medicare may cover you. But, if you have developed dementia or are looking to move to a nursing facility because you can no longer bathe, dress, toilet, feed yourself, or take care of your hygiene, etc., then Medicare is not going to pay for your nursing home costs.[8]

You can enroll in Medicare anytime during the three months before and three months after your sixty-fifth birthday. Miss your enrollment deadline, and you could risk paying increased premiums for the rest of your life.[9] On top of prompt enrollment, there are a few other things to think about when it comes to Medicare, not least among them being the need to understand the different "parts," what they do, and what they don't cover.

## Part A

Medicare Part A is what you might think of as "classic" Medicare. Hospital care, some types of home health care, and major medical care fall under this. While most enrollees pay nothing for this service (as they likely paid into the system for at least ten years), you may end up paying, either based on work history or delayed signup. In 2023, the highest premium is $506 per month, and a hospital stay does have a deductible, $1,600.[10] And, if you have a hospital stay that surpasses sixty days, you could be looking at additional costs; keep in mind, Medicare doesn't pay for long-term care and services.

---

[8] Medicare.gov. "What Part A covers." https://www.medicare.gov/what-medicare-covers/part-a/what-part-a-covers.html
[9] Medicare.gov. "When can I sign up for Medicare?" https://www.medicare.gov/basics/get-started-with-medicare/sign-up/when-can-i-sign-up-for-medicare
[10] Medicare. "Medicare 2023 Costs at a Glance." https://www.medicare.gov/your-medicare-costs/medicare-costs-at-a-glance

## Part B

Medicare Part B is an essential piece of wrap-around coverage for Medicare Part A. It helps pay for doctor visits and outpatient services. This also comes with a price tag: Although the Part B deductible is only $226 in 2023, you will still pay 20 percent of all costs after that, with no limit on out-of-pocket expenses. The Part B monthly premium for 2023 ranges from the standard amount of $164.90 to $560.50.[11]

## Part C

Medicare Part C, more commonly known as Medicare Advantage plans, are an alternative to a combination of Parts A, B, and sometimes D. Administered through private insurance companies, these have a variety of costs and restrictions, and they are subject to the specific policies and rules of the issuing carrier.

## Part D

Medicare Part D is also through a private insurer and is supplemental to Parts A and B, as its primary purpose is to cover prescription drugs. Like any private insurance plan, Part D has its quirks and rules that vary from insurer to insurer.

### The Donut Hole

Even with a "Part D" in place, you may still have a coverage gap between what your Part D private drug insurance pays for your prescription and what basic Medicare pays. In 2023, the coverage gap is $4,660, meaning, after you meet your private prescription insurance limit, you will spend no more than 25

---

[11] Ibid.

percent of your drug costs out-of-pocket before Medicare will kick in to pay for more prescription drugs.[12]

## Medicare Supplements

Medicare Supplement Insurance, MedSupp, Medigap, or plans labeled Medicare Part F, G, H, I, J . . . Known by a variety of monikers, this is just a fancy way of saying "medical coverage for those over sixty-five that picks up the tab for whatever the federal Medicare program(s) doesn't." Again, costs, limitations, etc., vary by carrier.

Does that sound like a bunch of government alphabet soup to you? It certainly does to me. And, did you read the fine print? Unpredictable costs, varied restrictions, difficult-to-compare benefits, donut holes, and coverage gaps. That's par for the course with health care plans through the course of our adult lives. What gives? I thought Medicare was supposed to be easier, comprehensive, and at no cost!

The truth is there is probably no stage of life when health care is easy to understand. I believe the most significant conversation with couples who want to retire before sixty-five is about the affordability of medical insurance before they qualify for Medicare. It's always fascinating to see the shock on their faces when we discuss the cost of health care for a couple in their sixties. Most people's medical premiums jump substantially from what they were paying, co-paying, or sharing with their current employers to paying out of pocket for the entire family.

The second thing is that when these couples finally get to Medicare, the different Medicare choices are confusing. Medicare Supplements help augment what Medicare provides. I always say I'm amused to explain Medicare Supplements by elaborating on parts A, B, C, D, E, F, G, H, I, and J. I call it the

---

[12] Medicare. "Costs in the coverage gap." https://www.medicare.gov/drug-coverage-part-d/costs-for-medicare-drug-coverage/costs-in-the-coverage-gap

alphabet soup of Medicare. There are so many different kinds of choices that it can make your head spin. Finding the right strategies for the right set of circumstances is a unique discussion for most families, and we help them to be able to decide what strategy fits them the best.

One of the best things you can do for yourself is to scope out the health care field early, compare costs often, and prepare for out-of-pocket costs well in advance—decades, if possible.

## *Medicaid*

Medicaid is a program the states administer, so funding, protocol, and limitations vary. Compared to Medicare, Medicaid more widely covers nursing home care, but it targets a different demographic: those with low incomes.

If you have more assets than the Medicaid limit in your state and need nursing home care, you will need to use those assets to pay for your care. You will also have a list of additional state-approved ways to spend some of these assets over the Medicaid limit, such as pre-purchasing burial plots and funeral expenses or paying off debts. After that, your remaining assets fund your nursing home stay until they are gone, at which point Medicaid will jump in.

Some people aren't stymied by this, thinking they will just pass on their financial assets early, gifting them to relatives, friends, and causes so they can qualify for Medicaid when they need it. However, to prevent this exact scenario, Uncle Sam has implemented the look-back period. Currently, if you enroll in Medicaid, you are subject to having the government scrutinize the last five years of your finances for large gifts or expenses that may subject you to penalties, temporarily making you ineligible for Medicaid coverage.

So, if you're planning to preserve your money for future generations and retain control of your financial resources during your lifetime, you'll probably want to prepare for the costs of longevity beyond a "government plan."

## *Self-Funding*

One way to fund a longer life is the old-fashioned way, through self-funding. There are a variety of financial tools you can use, and they all have their pros and cons. If your assets are in low-interest financial vehicles (savings, bonds, CDs), you risk letting inflation erode the value of your dollar. Or, if you are relying on the stock market, you have more growth potential, but you'll also want to consider the possible implications of market volatility. What if your assets take a hit? If you suffer a loss in your retirement portfolio in early or mid-retirement, you might have the option to "tighten your belt," so to speak, and cut back on discretionary spending to allow your portfolio the room to bounce back. But, if you are retired and depend on income from a stock account that just hit a downward stride, what are you going to do?

## *HSAs*

These days, you might also be able to self-fund through a health savings account, or HSA, if you have access to one through a high-deductible health plan (you will not qualify to save in an HSA after enrolling in Medicare). In an HSA, any growth of your tax-deductible contributions will be tax-free, and any distributions paid out for qualified health costs are also tax-free. Long-term care expenses count as health costs, so, if this is an option available to you, it is one way to use the tax advantages to self-fund your longevity. Bear in mind, if you are younger than sixty-five, any money you use for nonqualified expenses will be subject to taxes and penalties, and, if you are older than sixty-five, any HSA money you use for non-medical expenses is subject to income tax.

## *LTCI*

One slightly more nuanced way to pay for longevity, specifically for long-term care, is long-term care insurance, or LTCI. As car insurance protects your assets in case of a car accident and home insurance protects your assets in case something happens to your house, long-term care insurance aims to protect your assets in case you need long-term care in an at-home or nursing home situation.

As with other types of insurance, you will pay a monthly or annual premium in exchange for an insurance company paying for long-term care down the road. Typically, policies cover two to three years of care, which is adequate for an "average" situation: it's estimated 70 percent of Americans will need about three years of long-term care of some kind.

Now, there are a few oft-cited components of LTCI that make it unattractive for some:

- Expense — LTCI can be expensive. It is generally less expensive the younger you are, but a sixty-five-year-old couple who purchased LTCI in 2022 could expect to pay a combined amount of $3,750 each year for an average three-year coverage policy. And the annual cost only increases from there the older you are.[13]
- Limited options — Let's face it: LTCI may be expensive for consumers, but it can also be expensive for companies that offer it. With fewer companies willing to take on that expense, this narrows the market, meaning opportunities to price shop for policies with different options or custom benefits are limited.
- If you know you need it, you might not be able to get it — Insurance companies offering LTCI are taking on a risk that you may need LTCI. That risk is the foundation of the product—you may or may not need it. If you know you will need it because you have a dementia diagnosis or another illness for which you will need long-term care, you will likely not qualify for LTCI coverage.

---

[13] American Association for Long-Term Care Insurance. 2023. . "Long-Term Care Insurance Facts – Data – Statistics – 2022 Reports" https://www.aaltci.org/long-term-care-insurance/learning-center/ltcfacts-2022.php#2022costs-65

- Use it or lose it—If you have LTCI and are in the minority of Americans who die having never needed long-term care, all the money you paid into your LTCI policy is gone.
- Possibly fluctuating rates—Your rate is not locked in on LTCI. Companies maintain the ability to raise or lower your premium amounts. This means some seniors face an ultimatum: Keep funding a policy at what might be a less affordable rate *or* lose coverage and let go of all the money they paid in so far.

After that, you might be thinking, "How can people possibly be interested in LTCI?" But let me repeat myself—as many as 70 percent of Americans will need long-term care. And, although only one in ten Americans age fifty-five-plus have purchased LTCI, keep in mind the high cost of nursing home care. Can you afford $7,000 a month to put into nursing home care and still have enough left over to protect your legacy? This is a very real concern considering one set of statistics reported a two-in-three chance that a senior citizen will become physically or cognitively impaired in their lifetime.[14] So, not to sound like a broken record, but it is vitally important to have a plan in place to deal with longevity and long-term care if you intend to leave a financial legacy.

I sell long-term care insurance only because I'm passionate about helping protect a couple's financial life. The saddest reality is to see a couple being married forty, fifty, and even sixty years, and one of them becomes sick and needs care to help them through the day, whether at home or a nursing home. Because they love each other, they want to best care for each other without often counting the cost. The ill spouse knows they are spending down the wealth, and the remaining spouse knows it as well but puts their life mate ahead of themselves.

---

[14] payingforseniorcare.com. 2022. "Long-Term Senior Care Statistics" https://www.payingforseniorcare.com/statistics

Then the ill spouse passes, and the remaining spouse finds that some of the capital has been spent, and they are sometimes in a more precarious financial position. You lived and built wealth carefully over many years, only to find you could be dependent on your children at the end of your life just because you ignored planning for long-term care. It can be a somber story and one that could have been avoided with better planning and not ignoring this potentially large risk.

A few relevant statistics to keep in mind:
- The longer you live, the more likely you are to continue living; the longer you live, the more health care you will likely need to pay for.
- The average cost of a private nursing home room in the United States in 2021 was $9,034 a month.[15] But keep in mind, that is just the nursing home—it doesn't include other medical costs, let alone pleasantries, like entertainment or hobby spending.
- In 2022, Fidelity calculated that a healthy couple retiring at age sixty-five could expect to pay around $315,000 over the course of retirement to cover health and medical expenses.

I know. Whoa, there, Hilgardt, I was hoping to have a realistic idea of health costs, not be driven over by a cement mixer!

The good news is, while we don't know these exact costs in advance, we know there *will* be costs. And you won't have to pay your total Medicare lifetime premiums in one day as a lump sum. Now that you have a good idea of health care costs in retirement, you can *plan* for them! That's the real point, here: Planning in advance can keep you from feeling nickel-and-dimed to your wits' end. Instead, having a sizeable portion of your assets earmarked for health care can allow you the

---

[15] Genworth Financial. January 31, 2022. "Genworth 2020 Cost of Care Survey." https://www.genworth.com/aging-and-you/finances/cost-of-care.html

freedom to choose health care networks, coverage options, and long-term care possibilities you like and that you think offer you the best in life.

## *Product Riders*

LTCI and self-funding are not the only ways to plan for the expenses of longevity. Some companies are getting creative with their products, particularly insurance companies. One way they are retooling to meet people's needs is through optional product riders on annuities and life insurance. Elsewhere in this book, I talk about annuity basics, but here's a brief overview: Annuities are insurance contracts. You pay the insurance company a premium, either as a lump sum or as a series of payments over a set amount of time, in exchange for guaranteed income payments. One of the advantages of an annuity is it has access to riders, which allow you to tweak your contract for a fee, usually about 1 percent of the contract value annually. One annuity rider some companies offer is a long-term care rider. If you have an annuity with a long-term care rider and are not in need of long-term care, your contract behaves as any annuity contract would—nothing changes. Generally speaking, if you reach a point when you can't perform multiple functions of daily life on your own, you notify the insurance company, and a representative will turn on those provisions of your contract.

Like LTCI, different companies and products offer different options. Some annuity long-term care riders offer coverage of two years in a nursing home situation. Others cap expenses at two times the original annuity's value. It greatly depends. Some people prefer this option because there isn't a "use-it-or-lose-it" piece; if you die without ever having needed long-term care, you still will have had the income benefit from the base contract. Still, as with any annuities or insurance contracts, there are the usual restrictions and limitations. Withdrawing money from the contract will affect future income payments, early distributions can result in a penalty, income taxes may apply, and, because the insurance company's solvency is what guarantees your payments, it's important to do your research about the insurance company you are considering purchasing a contract from.

Understandably, a discussion on long-term care is bound to feel at least a little tedious. Yet, this is an important piece of planning for income in retirement, particularly if you want to leave a legacy. I like to start discussing long-term care when people are in their fifties, when their health is usually still good, and premiums are generally more affordable. Of course, not everyone is open to having this discussion. It's an easy one to put off when you assume your health will be good for years, maybe even decades, to come. This can be a gamble I believe most people shouldn't take.

Let's look at a fictional couple, Jack and Jane, who are both in their early fifties and still in good health. At age fifty-two, they already have enough saved to retire. Jack and Jane don't want to think about getting older and possibly getting sick, so they put off planning for it. Sadly, when Jack is fifty-four, he is diagnosed with an aggressive version of Alzheimer's. Suddenly, their future is uncertain.

For several years, Jane provided her husband with the best care she can afford, but the expense is much greater than expected. After five years, Jack passes away, leaving Jane emotionally and financially unstable. Jane is now in her late fifties, with limited funds, and still has a potentially long life ahead. Sadly, with proper planning, her situation could have been avoided.

I have seen people go through situations like this too many times, and the biggest lesson I have learned is that even relatively young people in good health should consider this kind of care and planning. We can't predict the future, but we can prepare for it.

# Spousal Planning

Here's one thing to keep in mind no matter how you plan to save: Many of us will be planning for more than ourselves. Look back at all the stats on health events and the likelihood of long life and long-term care. If they hold true for a single individual, then the likelihood of having a costly health or long-term care event is even higher for a married couple. You'll be planning for not just one life, but two. So, when it comes to long-term care insurance, annuities, self-funding, or whatever strategy you are looking at using, be sure you are funding longevity for the both of you.

CHAPTER 2

# Taxes

Where to begin with taxes? Perhaps by acknowledging we all bear responsibility for the resources we share. Roads, bridges, schools . . . It is the patriotic duty of every American to pay their fair share of taxes. Many would agree with me. However, while they don't mind paying their fair share, they're not interested in paying one cent more than that!

Now, just talking taxes probably takes your mind to April—tax season. You are probably thinking about all the forms you collect and how you file. Perhaps you are thinking about your certified public accountant or another qualified tax professional and saying to yourself, "I've already got taxes taken care of, thanks!"

However, what I see when people come into my office is that their relationship with their tax professional is purely a January through April relationship. That means they may have a tax professional, but not a tax *planner*.

What I mean is tax planning extends beyond filing taxes. In April, we are required to settle our accounts with the IRS to make sure we have paid up on our bill or to even the score if we have overpaid. But real tax planning is about making each financial move in a way that allows you to keep the most money in your pocket and out of Uncle Sam's.

As a caveat, I want to emphasize that I am neither a CPA nor a tax return preparer, but I see how taxes affect my clients. I have plenty of experience helping clients implement tax-efficient strategies in their retirement plans in conjunction with their tax professionals.

Over the years, I have been able to work with CPAs and tax attorneys for wealthy families and high-income earning business owners. I'm always astounded by the quality of planning and the amount of taxes that can potentially be avoided when these three professionals fully understand the family's past, current, and future situation.

In working with CPAs and tax attorneys, we center on approximately forty concepts that can help our families with income tax reduction and the reduction and even possible avoidance of capital gains tax and estate taxes. Working and thinking together has been very rewarding for our clients. It is especially important to me to help my clients develop tax-efficient strategies in their retirement plans because each dollar they can keep in their pockets is a dollar we can put to work.

When I first studied the United States tax code, I was astonished to note that a client can invest in the same exchange-traded fund with the same return and have three different results, all based on which tax environment this ETF is in. Wealth growing in a taxable environment can often be the least tax efficient strategy. Increasing wealth in a tax-deferred environment can improve efficiency, but a tax-free environment can ultimately be the most efficient one. The sad news is that, in my experience, most families' wealth is in the tax-deferred or taxable buckets.

A common reason for this is a lack of understanding of the choices available to a family. We focus on measuring a family's tax liability between now and their children inheriting the money. When a family sees the potential result of their tax liability, they often become ready to start planning to make improvements. The ultimate strategy lies in the detailed planning of their retirement cash flow. The source of the income streams in retirement determines the total tax liability in any given year. In other words, what taxable environments the cash flow gets distributed from can influence the tax bill.

Also, the kind of income tax deduction strategy that we help create can influence the tax bill. Tax planning can be done when the plans of a family are very well understood, as I said before.

A potentially large tax often overlooked is the income tax due when your family inherits wealth. An example is income tax on the inheritance of IRAs. This is called an IRD tax, income in respect of a decedent. This can also be reduced strategically through planning.

## The Fed

Now, in the United States, taxes can be a rather uncertain proposition. Depending on who is in the White House and which party controls Congress, we might be tempted to assume tax rates could either decline or increase in the next four to eight years accordingly. However, there is one (large!) factor we, as a nation, must confront: the national debt.

Currently, according to USDebtClock.org, we are over $31,000,000,000,000 in debt and climbing. That's $31 *trillion* with a "T." With just $1 trillion, you could park it in the bank at a zero percent interest rate and spend more than $54 million every day for fifty years without hitting a zero balance.

Even if Congress got a handle and stopped that debt from its daily compound, divided by each taxpayer, we each would owe about $246,000. So, will that be check, cash, or Venmo?[16]

My point here isn't to give you anxiety. I'm just cautioning you that even with the rosiest of outlooks on our personal income tax rates, none of us should count on low tax rates for the long term. Instead, you and your network of professionals (tax, legal, and financial) should constantly be looking for ways to take advantage of tax-saving opportunities as they come. After all, the best "luck" is when proper planning meets opportunity.

So, how can we get started?

---

[16] usdebtclock.org.

# Know Your Limits

One of the foundational pieces of tax planning is knowing what tax bracket you are in, based on your income after subtracting pre-tax or untaxed assets. Your income taxes are based on your taxable income.

One reason to know your taxable income and your income tax rate is so you can see how far away you are from the next lower or higher tax bracket. This is particularly important when it comes to decisions such as gifting and Roth IRA rollovers.

For instance, when confronting the 2022 federal income tax return they filed in 2023, Mallory and Ralph's taxable income is just over $345,000, putting them in the 32 percent tax bracket and about $4,900 above the upper end of the 24 percent tax bracket. They have already maxed out their retirement funds' tax-exempt contributions for the year. Their daughter, Gloria, is a sophomore in college. This couple could shave a considerable amount off their tax bill if they use the $4,900 to help Gloria out with groceries and school—something they were likely to do, anyway, but now can deliberately be put to work for them in their overall financial strategy.

Now, I use Mallory and Ralph only as an example—your circumstances are probably different—but I think this nicely illustrates the way planning ahead for taxes can save you money.

## Assuming a Lower Tax Rate

Many people anticipate being in a lower tax bracket in retirement. It makes sense: You won't be contributing to retirement funds; you'll be drawing from them. And you won't have all those work expenses—work clothes, transportation, lunch meetings, etc.

Yet, do you really plan on changing your lifestyle after retirement? Do you plan to cut down on the number of times you eat out, scale back vacations, and skimp on travel?

What I see in my office is many couples spend more in the first few years, or maybe the first decade, of retirement. Sure, that may taper off later on, but usually only just in time for their budget to be hit with greater health and long-term care expenses. Do you see where this is going? Many people plan as though their taxable income will be lower in retirement and are surprised when the tax bills come in and look more or less the same as they used to. It's better to plan for the worst and hope for the best, wouldn't you agree?

# 401(k)/IRA

One sometimes-unexpected piece of tax planning in retirement concerns your 401(k) or IRA. Most of us have one of these accounts or an equivalent. Throughout our working lives, we pay in, dutifully socking away a portion of our earnings in these tax-deferred accounts. There's the rub: tax-deferred. Not tax-free. Very rarely is anything free of taxation when you get down to it. Using 401(k)s and IRAs in retirement is no different. The taxes the government deferred when you were in your working years are now coming due, and you will pay taxes on that income at whatever your current tax rate is.

Just to ensure Uncle Sam gets his due, the government also has a required minimum distribution, or RMD, rule. Beginning at age seventy-two, you are required to withdraw a certain minimum amount every year from your 401(k) or IRA, or else you will face a tax penalty on any RMD monies you should have withdrawn but didn't—and that's on top of income tax. The SECURE Act 2.0 reduced the penalty to 25 percent (from 50 percent). Timely corrections also can reduce the penalty to 10 percent. [17]

---

[17] Jim Probasco. Investopedia.com. January 6, 2023. "SECURE 2.0 Act of 2022." https://www.investopedia.com/secure-2-0-definition-5225115

Of course, there is also the Roth account. You can think of the difference between a Roth and a traditional retirement account as the difference between taxing the seed and taxing the harvest. Because Roths are funded with post-tax dollars, there aren't tax penalties for early withdrawals of the principal nor are there taxes on the growth after you reach age fifty-nine-and-one-half. Perhaps best of all, there are no RMDs. Of course, you must own a Roth account for a minimum of five years before you are able to take advantage of all its features.

This is one more area where it pays to be aware of your tax bracket. Some people may find it advantageous to "convert" their traditional retirement account funds to Roth account funds in a year during which they are in a lower tax bracket. Others may opt to put any excess RMDs from their traditional retirement accounts into other products, like stocks or insurance.

Does that make your head spin? Understandable. That's why it's so important to work with a financial professional and tax planner who can help you execute these sorts of tax-efficient strategies and help you understand what you are doing and why.

"There are two systems of taxation in our country: One for the informed and one for the uninformed. This famous quote from Judge Learned Hand, a former federal judge on the Second Circuit US Court of Appeals, is very interesting and true. The tax code is complicated, and when you include all the regulations and guidance, it consists of about seventy-five thousand pages.

This is where it can be important to distinguish between the experience and quality of advisors you have. A combination of a forward-thinking CPA and a comprehensive planning advisor can help you reduce your tax liability, perhaps substantially. A financial planning advisor can help the family discover their vision for the future—all the way until wealth is inherited, which will equip both professionals to deploy tax-efficient strategies for the family. Translation: the potential for substantial tax savings.

CHAPTER 3

# Market Volatility

U p and down. Roller coaster. Merry-go-round. Bulls and bears. Peak-to-trough.

Sound familiar? This is the language we use to talk about the stock market. With volatility and spikes, even our language is jarring, bracing, and vivid.

Still, financial strategies tend to revolve around market-based products, for good reasons. For one thing, there is no other financial class that packs the same potential for growth, pound for pound, as stock-based products. Because of growth potential, inflation preservation, and new opportunities, it may be unwise to avoid the market entirely.

However, along with the potential for growth is the potential for loss. At the time this book was written, many of the people I've seen in my office came in feeling uneasy because of the economic fallout of the COVID-19 outbreak of 2020, followed by the economic downturn, and the inflation spike that happened in 2022.

So how do we balance these factors? How do we try to satisfy both the need for protection and the need for growth?

For one thing, it is important to recognize the value of diversity. Now, I'm not just talking about the diversity of assets among different kinds of stocks, or even different kinds of stocks and bonds. That's only one kind of diversity; while important, both stocks and bonds, though different, are both still market-based products. Most market-based products, even within a diverse portfolio, tend to rise or lower as a whole, just like an incoming tide. Therefore, a portfolio diverse in only market-sourced products won't automatically preserve your assets during times when the market declines.

In addition to the sort of "horizontal diversity" you have by purchasing a variety of stocks and bonds from different companies, I also suggest you think about "vertical diversity," or diversity among asset classes. This means having different product types, including securities products, bank products, and insurance products—with varying levels of growth potential, liquidity, and protection—all in accordance with your unique situation, goals, and needs.

The first challenge can be finding an advisor or broker that has full knowledge of the products offered by these three institutions. You see, traditionally, brokers representing an institution learn how to sell what the institution offers and often how to point out the negatives of the offerings of other institutions. This can create the challenge of not having the opportunity to fully understand the pros and cons of different strategies.

Most families are looking for independent and objective advice on all the strategies regardless of where they came from. When you fully understand your choices, you are intelligent to see what approach you prefer or even what combination of approaches works the best in your unique situation. There is no perfect investment. We often find the right strategy is in unique combinations of products.

The second challenge can be determining the combined risk tolerance of a husband and wife. To accomplish this, we use a wonderful computer software tool called Riskalyze. It is a very interesting questionnaire the husband and wife take, and the score comes in separately. It always provokes healthy conversation, especially when the scores come back as opposites. We then determine the combined score and why unity as a couple can be more important for the marriage than beating an index.

Thirdly, probably one of the biggest eye-openers is to evaluate the risk that should be taken to help them accomplish their retirement plan. Acceptable investment risk is a large factor in finding the financial plan you love. If the risk needs to be reduced, the couple may need to agree upon a later retirement date, for example.

# The Color of Money

When you're looking at the overall diversity of your portfolio, part of the equation is knowing which products fit in what category: what has liquidity, what has protection, and what has growth potential.

Before we dive in, keep in mind these aren't absolutes. You might think of liquidity, growth, and protection as primary colors. While some products will look pretty much yellow, red, or blue, others will have a mix of characteristics, making them more green, orange, or purple.

## Growth

I like to think of the growth category as red. It's powerful, it's somewhat volatile, and it's also the category where we have the greatest opportunities for growth and loss. Often, products in the growth category will have a good deal of liquidity but very little protection. These are our market-based products and strategies, and we think of them mostly in shades of red and orange, to designate their growth and liquidity. This is a good place to be when you're young—think fast cars and flashy leather jackets—but its allure often wanes as you move closer to retirement. Examples of "red" products include:

- Stocks
- Equities
- Exchange-traded funds
- Mutual funds
- Corporate bonds
- Real estate investment trusts
- Speculations

- Alternative investments

## Liquidity

Yellow is my liquid category color. I typically recommend having at least enough yellow money to cover six months to a year's worth of expenses in case of emergency. Yellow assets don't need a lot of growth potential; they just need to be readily available when we need them. The "yellow" category includes assets like:
- Cash
- Money market accounts

## Protection

The color of protection, to me, is blue. Tranquil, peaceful, sure, even if it lacks a certain amount of flash. This is the direction I like to see people generally move toward as they're nearing retirement. The red, flashy look of stock market returns and the risk of possible overnight losses is less attractive as we near retirement and look for more consistency and reliability. While this category doesn't come with a lot of liquidity, the products here are backed by an insurance company, a bank, or a government entity. "Blue" products include things such as:
- Certificates of deposit (backed by banks)
- Government-based bonds (backed by the U.S. government)
- Life insurance (backed by insurance companies)
- Annuities (backed by insurance companies)

Our unique philosophy regarding different investment vehicles is that no one investment is perfect. A comprehensive financial plan gives you the proper context to evaluate the right combination of investment vehicles for your distinct scenario.

The time until you need to turn the investment asset into cash flow is a significant factor in analyzing what strategies are the right fit. Generally, the longer your timeframe, the more risk you can afford to take, all things being equal. It typically takes time to determine the volatility in the returns of market-related investments.

# 401(k)s

I want to take a second to specifically address a product many retirees will be using to build their retirement income: the 401(k) and other retirement accounts. Any of these retirement accounts (IRAs, 401(k)s, 403(b)s, etc.) are basically "tax wrappers." What do I mean by that? Well, depending on your plan provider, a 401(k) could include target-date funds, passively managed products, stocks, bonds, mutual funds, or even variable, fixed, and fixed index annuities, all collected in one place and governed by rules (a.k.a. the "tax wrapper"). These rules govern how much money you can put inside, what ways you can put it in, when you will pay taxes on it, and when you can take the money out. Inside the 401(k), each of the products inside the "tax wrapper" might have its own fees or commissions, in addition to the management fee you pay on the 401(k) itself.

Now, fees can be troublesome. You can't get something for nothing, and fees are how many financial companies and professionals make a living. Yet, it's important to recognize even a fee with a fraction of a percentage point is money out of your pocket—money that represents not just the one-time fee of today but also represents an opportunity cost. For example, consider a $100,000 IRA that earns 6 percent over a twenty-five-year period without investment fees would earn $430,000. But if just a 0.5 percent fee got factored into that investment, the IRA would be worth $379,000 in twenty-five years, a $50,500 decrease.[18] For someone close to retirement, how much do you think fees may have cost over their lifetime?

---

[18] Pam Krueger. Kiplinger.com. January 8, 2021. "How to Spot (and Squash) Nasty Fees That Hide in Your Investments" https://www.kiplinger.com/retirement/retirement-planning/602043/how-to-spot-and-squash-nasty-fees-that-hide-in-your

Even for those close to retirement, it's important to look at management fees and assess if you think you're getting what you pay for. Over the course of ten years, those costs can add up, and you may have decades ahead of you in which you will need to rely on your assets.

## Dollar-Cost Averaging

With 401(k)s and other market-based retirement products, dollar-cost averaging is a concept that can work in your favor when you are investing for the long term. When the market is trending up, if you are consistently paying in money, month over month, great; your investments can grow, and you are adding to your assets. When the market takes a dip, no problem; your dollars buy more shares at a lower price. At some point, we hope the market will rebound, in which case your shares can grow and possibly be more valuable than they were before. This concept is what we call "dollar-cost averaging." While it can't ensure a profit or guarantee against losses, it's a time-tested strategy for investing in a volatile market.

However, when you are in retirement, this strategy may work against you. You may have heard of "reverse" dollar-cost averaging. Before, when the market lost ground, you were "bargain-shopping"; your dollars purchased more assets at a reduced price. When you are in retirement, you are no longer the purchaser; you are selling. So, in a down market, you have to sell more assets to make the same amount of money as what you made in a favorable market.

I've had lots of people step into my office to talk to me about this, emphasizing, "my advisor says the market always bounces back, and I have to just hold on for the long term."

There's some basis for this thinking; thus far, the market has always rebounded to higher heights than before. But this is no guarantee, and the prospect of potentially higher returns in five years may not be very helpful in retirement if you are relying on the income from those returns to pay this month's electric bill, for example.

The way we address market volatility is to put market volatility in the right place when we plan for a family's income in retirement. Lifetime Income can be derived from one of three sources—guaranteed income sources like Social Security, pensions, or annuity contracts with income guarantees and/or principal guarantees.

The second area is income that is produced by the underlying investments. Examples would be interest from bonds and dividends from stocks. We call these yield-oriented investments.

The third kind of income is when we are systematically selling a growth-orientated investment.

When creating a detailed cash flow plan, we often use all three sources. Again, our clients are looking for the right context when deciding how much of their income will come from different sources.

Many make the mistake of investing and hoping for the best. In fact, most families who become our clients do not have a detailed financial plan and usually do not have the confidence that their money will last a lifetime. Their current brokers have not always taken the time or do not know how to plan and illustrate the probability of success.

Families also need to understand one of the biggest risks they can encounter at their phase of life. It is called the sequence of returns risk. This is a risk when you are in the spend-down stage of life and can reverse your retirement if not planned for carefully.

This example very simply explains it: If a client has $1,000,000 that needs to produce an income of $50,000, and the markets are down by 20 percent, the million dollars go down to $800,000 and then the income distribution of $50,000 and the balance at the end of the year is $750,000.

Now, what is the chance that this account will ever grow back to $1 million if, in the next year, another $50,000 has to be distributed for lifestyle? Sometimes, depending on the market returns in the future, the balance never returns to $1 million, and the future sustainability of the $50,000 income distribution becomes unsustainable. This can become especially concerning if we experience two or three consequential negative years in the markets.

It's a potentially big risk that many people do not seem to know about the effect of the sequence of returns risk. They simply trust others who just say, "Don't; worry it will work out." And then are very disappointed that it did not work out for them. Today, we have sophisticated tools to help assess this risk for you, and they can help you reduce this risk and potentially improve the chances of success that the money will last a lifetime.

## Is There a "Perfect" Product?

To bring us back around to the discussion of protection, growth, and liquidity, the ideal product would be a "ten" in all three categories, right? Completely guaranteed, doubling in size every few years, and accessible whenever you want. Does such a product exist? Absolutely not.

Instead of running in circles looking for that perfect product, the silver bullet, the unicorn of financial strategies, it's more important to circle back to the concept of a balanced, asset-diverse portfolio.

This is why your interests may be better served when you work with a knowledgeable financial professional who knows what various financial products can do and how to use them in your personal retirement strategy.

\* Investing involves risk, including the potential loss of principal. No investment strategy can guarantee a profit or protect against loss in periods of declining values. Any references to protection benefits or guaranteed/lifetime income streams refer only to fixed insurance products, not securities or investment products. Insurance and annuity product guarantees are backed by the financial strength and claims-paying ability of the issuing insurance company.

Insurance products are offered through the insurance business The LifeWealth Group. The LifeWealth Group is also an Investment Advisory practice that offers products and services through AE Wealth Management, LLC (AEWM), a Registered Investment Advisor. AEWM does not offer insurance products. The insurance products offered by The LifeWealth Group are not subject to investment Advisor requirements.

CHAPTER 4

# Retirement Income

Retirement. For many of us, it's what we've saved for and dreamed of, pinning our hopes to a magical someday. Is that someday full of traveling? Is it filled with grandkids? Gardening? Maybe your fondest dream is simply never having to work again, never having to clock in or be accountable to someone else.

Your ability to do these things all hinges on *income*. Without the money to support these dreams, even a basic level of work-free lifestyle is unsustainable. That's why planning for your income in retirement is so foundational. But where do we begin?

It's easy to feel overwhelmed by this question. Some may feel the urge to amass a large lump sum and then try to put it all in one product—insurance, investments, liquid assets—to provide all the growth, liquidity, and income they need. Instead, I think you need a more balanced approach. After all, retirement planning isn't magic. Like I mention elsewhere, there is no single product that can be all things to all people (or even all things to one person). No approach works unilaterally for everyone. That's why it's important to talk to a financial professional who can help you lay down the basics and take you step-by-step through the process. Not only will you have the assurance you have addressed the areas you need to, but you will also have an ally who can help you break down the process and help keep you from feeling overwhelmed.

# Sources of Income

Thinking of all the pieces of your retirement expenses might be intimidating. But, like cleaning out a junk drawer or revisiting that garage remodel, once you have laid everything out, you can begin to sort things into categories.

Once you have a good overall picture of where your expenses will lie, you can start stacking up the resources to cover them.

## Social Security

Social Security is a guaranteed, inflation-protected federal insurance program playing a significant part in most of our retirement plans. From delaying until you've reached full retirement age or beyond to examining spousal benefits, as I discuss elsewhere in this book, there is plenty you can do to try to make the most of this monthly benefit. As with all your retirement income sources, it's important to consider how to make this resource stretch to provide the most bang and buck for your situation.

## Pension

Another generally reliable source of retirement income for you might be a pension, if you are one of the lucky people who still has one.

If you don't have a pension, go ahead and skim on to the next section. If you do have a pension, keep on reading.

Because your pension can be such a central piece of your retirement income plan, you will want to put some thought into answering basic questions about it.

How well is your pension funded? Since the heyday of the pension plan, companies and governments have neglected to fund their pension obligations, causing a persistent problem with this otherwise reliable asset. However, research conducted by the Pew Charitable Trusts showed a collective increase in assets exceeding half a trillion dollars in state retirement plans fueled by strong market investment returns in fiscal 2021. Pew's estimates that state retirement systems rose to 80 percent funding for the first time in 2008.[19]

Consider the factors at play, though. Pensions had been underfunded and gained a boost from strong market performance in 2021. What happens to the solvency of those pension funds if the market declines?

It can be worthwhile to keep tabs on your pension's health and know what your options are for withdrawing your pension. If you have already retired and made those decisions, this may be a foregone conclusion. If not, it pays to know what you can expect and what decisions you can make, such as taking spousal options to cover your husband or wife if he or she outlives you.

Also, some companies are incentivizing lump-sum payouts of pensions to reduce the companies' payment liabilities. If that's the case with your employer, talk to your financial professional to see if it might be prudent to do something like that or if it might be better to stick with lifetime payments or other options.

## Your 401(k) and IRA

One "modern way" to save for retirement is in a 401(k) or IRA (or their nonprofit or governmental equivalents). These tax-advantaged accounts are, in my opinion, a poor substitute for pensions, but one of the biggest disservices we do to ourselves is to not take full advantage of them in the first place. According to one article, only 41 percent of Americans invest in a 401(k),

---

[19] pewtrusts.org. September 14, 2021. "The State Pension Funding Gap: Plans Have Stabilized in Wake of Pandemic" https://www.pewtrusts.org/en/research-and-analysis/issue-briefs/2021/09/the-state-pension-funding-gap-plans-have-stabilized-in-wake-of-pandemic

though 68 percent of employed Americans have access to a 401(k) benefit option.[20]

Also, if you have changed jobs over the years, do the work of tracking down any benefits from your past employers. You might have an IRA here or a 401(k) there; keep track of those so you can pull them together and look at those assets when you're ready to look at establishing sources of retirement income.

## Do You Have...

- Life insurance?
- Annuities?
- Long-term care insurance?
- Any passive income sources?
- Stock and bond portfolios?
- Liquid assets? (What's in your bank account?)
- Alternative investments?
- Rental properties?

If you are going through the work of sitting with a financial professional, it's important to look at your full retirement income picture and pull together *all* your assets, no matter how big or small. From the free insurance policy offered at your bank to the sizable investment in your brother-in-law's modestly successful furniture store, you want to have a good idea of where your money is.

"I am a millionaire, a multimillionaire!" Clark exclaimed. This often happens in our planning sessions with families when we pull together all the assets they have. Most people have not seen it all organized on one sheet of paper, and it is delightful to see how well they have saved for their futures.

---

[20] Amin Dabit. personalcapital.com. April 1, 2021. "The Average 401k Balance by Age." https://www.personalcapital.com/blog/retirement-planning/average-401k-balance-age/

During our session on creating the "plan you love," we can see how the saved assets play into the annual income they desire and if this is enough for a lifetime. This is truly the first time for most to view a picture of their current and future money, and it is exhilarating to see.

## Retirement Income Needs

How much income will you need in retirement? How do you determine that? A lot of people work toward a random number, thinking, "If I can just have a million dollars, I'll be comfortable in retirement!" Don't get me wrong; it is possible to save up a lot of money and then retire in the hopes you can keep your monthly expenses lower than some set estimation. But I think this carries a general risk of running out of money. Instead, I work with my clients to find out what their current and projected income needs are and then work from there to see how we might cover any gaps between what they have and what they want.

### Goals and Dreams

I like to start with your pie in the sky. Do you find yourself planning for your vacations more thoroughly than you do your retirement? It's not uncommon for Americans to spend more time planning our vacations than we spend planning our retirements. Maybe it's because planning a vacation is less stressful: Having a week at the beach go awry is, well, a walk on the beach compared to running out of money in retirement. Whatever the case, perhaps it would be better if you thought of your retirement as a vacation in and of itself—no clocking in, no boss, no overtime. If you felt unlimited by financial strain, what would you do?

Would an endless vacation for you mean Paris and Rome? Would it mean mentoring at children's clubs or serving at the local soup kitchen? Or maybe it would mean deepening your ties to those immediately around you—neighbors, friends, and family. Maybe it would mean more time to take part in the hobbies and activities you love. Have you been considering a second (or even third) act as a small-business owner, turning a hobby or passion into a revenue source?

This is your time to daydream and answer the question: If you could do anything, what would you do?

After that, it's a matter of putting a dollar amount on it. What are the costs of round-the-world travel? One couple I know said their highest priority in retirement was being able to take each of their grandchildren on a cross-country vacation every year. That's a pretty specific goal—one that is reasonably easy to nail down a budget for.

A couple let's call them, Phil and Jackie were referred to me by their CPA, about three years before Jackie's company sold out. She was the human resources director of her company, and they had a big dream about transitioning to the mountains of North Carolina in their retirement years to build their dream home. It took them two years to complete the construction of their mountain house. We took a picture of it and framed it on our "Dream Wall" to celebrate with them the accomplishment of this dream. My wife and I also had the joy of visiting Phil and Jackie in North Carolina.

As their lives transitioned, we discussed what their next adventure would look like. Jackie was passionate about helping stray dogs and cats, so she founded an animal shelter where they nurture and care for them until they find adoptive families. They have truly transitioned to their next passion and adventure in a beautiful area and home.

Another couple let's call them, Kevin and Lisa, came to us from a group they had started. They invited me to be a part of the group, and I love it. The group is called Dream Builders, and its purpose is to inspire people to pursue their God-given dreams. Now you understand why I love this group so much.

Kevin and Lisa also became clients, and we planned their retirement together. During this time, Kevin transitioned from a corporate career to becoming a branding consultant—a big part of his dream. All was set and moving along well. One day, I got a call from Kennan stating they decided to adopt the child they had been fostering.

Kevin and Lisa have two children of their own. They adopted another child, let's call him Brad, in their late fifties. It was very exciting but also challenging for the retirement plan as we had laid it out.

We met and pushed the goalpost out some years to make space for Brad. Now, we are tracking again for the future life they desire. But they cannot imagine a current life without Brad. What a blessing to see the impact of Kevin and Lisa. They also are on our Dream Wall of Fame.

## Current Budget

Compiling a current expense report is one of the trickiest pieces of retirement preparation. Many people assume the expenses of their lives in retirement will be different—lower. After all, there will be no drive to work, no need for a formal wardrobe, and, perhaps most impactful of all, no more saving for retirement!

Yet, we often underestimate our daily spending habits. That's why I typically ask my clients to bring in their bank statements for the past year—they are reflective of your *actual* spending, not just what you think you're spending.

Helping a family understand their income needs has a lot to do with helping a family understand their expenses at the moment. The way we do that is by creating a spending plan. I have found over the years that most families do not have a spending plan, which is one of the most profound tool we have to help a family optimize their wealth.

Spending plans empower people when they see their income and expenses and whether they like what they see. From here, they can make the necessary adjustments.

I can't count the number of times I have sat with a couple, asked them about their spending, and heard them throw out a number that seemed incredibly low. When I ask them where the number came from, they usually say they estimated based on their total bills. Yet, our spending is so much more than our mortgage, utilities, cable, phone, car, grocery, or credit card bills.

"What about clothes?" I ask, "Or dining out? What about gifts and coffees and last-minute birthday cards?" That's when the lights come on.

This is why I suggest collecting a year's worth of information. There is usually no such thing as a one-time purchase. Did you buy new furniture? Even if that is a rarity, do you think that will be the last time you *ever* buy furniture?

I recently started working with a couple that owns a business. The owner paid himself a variable income every month and felt strapped for cash all the time. His business was doing good, but it had so many moving parts, and managing the cash flow at work and at home was exhausting.

The couple had substantial credit card debts and were quite alarmed when they discovered how high the interest rates were. Because of the variable monthly income, they also accrued debt on their line of credit against their home.

They were alarmed that they could not point to one or two expenses that created that debt but that it was a monthly variable amount that accrued over time. The realization was painful, but it was the beginning of awareness and change. That change brought about a whole new spending pattern that put them in the position to work towards an exciting future. Yes, it will take some time to become debt-free. But most often, teamwork strengthens a marriage and a family. This strength can help lead to aggressive savings toward a stronger financial future. I am very proud to watch our families work to achieve their goals.

Another hefty expense is spending on the kids. Many of the couples I work with are quick to help their adult children, whether it's something like letting them live in the basement, paying for college, babysitting, paying an occasional bill, or contributing to a grandchild's college fund. Research concluded that 22 percent of adults receive some financial support from parents. That segment jumps to almost 30 percent when factoring the millennial generation.[21]

My clients sometimes protest that what they do for their grown children can stop in retirement. They don't *need* to help. But I get it. Parents like to feel needed. And, while you never want to neglect saving for retirement in favor of taking on financial risks (like your child's student debt), the parents who help their adult children do so in part because it helps them feel fulfilled.

When it comes down to expenses, including (and especially) spending on your family, don't make your initial calculations based on what you *could* whittle your budget down to if you *had* to. Instead, start from where you are. Who wants to live off a bare-bones bank account in retirement?

# Other Expenses

Once you have nailed down your current budget and your dreams or goals for retirement, there are a few other outstanding pieces to think about—some expenses many people don't take the time to consider before making and executing a plan. But I'm assuming you want to get it right, so let's take a look.

# Housing

Do you know where you want to live in retirement? This makes up a substantial piece of your income puzzle—since the typical American household owns a home, and it's generally their largest asset.

Some people prefer to live right where they are for as long as they can. Others have been waiting for retirement to pull the

---

[21] Kamaron McNair. magnifymoney.com. October 26, 2021. "Nearly 30% of Millennials Still Receive Financial Support From Their Parents" https://www.magnifymoney.com/blog/news/parental-financial-support-survey/

trigger on an ambitious move, like purchasing a new house, or even downsizing. Whatever your plans and whatever your reasons, there are quite a few things to consider.

## *Mortgage*

Do you still have a mortgage? What may have been a nice tax boon in your working years could turn into a financial burden in your retirement. After all, when you are on a limited income, a mortgage is just one more bill sapping your financial strength. It is something to put some thought into, whether you plan to age in place or are considering moving to your dream home, buying a house out of state, or living in a retirement community.

## *Upkeep and Taxes*

A house without a mortgage still requires annual taxes. While it's tempting to think of this as a once-a-year expense, when you have limited earning potential, your annual tax bill might be something into which you should put a little more forethought.

The costs of homeownership aren't just monetary. When you find yourself dealing with more house than you need, it can drain your time and energy. From keeping clutter at bay to keeping the lawn mower running, upkeep can be extensive and expensive. For some, that's a challenge they heartily accept and can comfortably take on. For others, the idea of yard work or cleaning an area larger than they need feels foolish.

For instance, Peggy discovered after her knee replacement that most of her house was inaccessible to her when she was laid up.

"It felt ridiculous to pay someone else to dust and vacuum a house I was only living in 40 percent of!"

## *Practicality and Adaptability*

Erik and Magda are looking to retire within the next two decades. They just sold their old three-bedroom ranch-style house. Their twins are in high school, and the couple has wanted to "upgrade" for years. Now they live in a gorgeous 1940s three-story house with all the kitchen space they ever wanted, five sprawling bedrooms, and a library and media room for themselves and their children. Within months of moving in, the couple realized a house perfect for their active teens would no longer be perfect for them in five to fifteen years.

"We are paying the mortgage for this house, but we've started saving for the next one," said Magda, "because who wants to climb two flights of stairs to their bedroom when they're seventy-eight?"

Others I know have encountered a similar situation in their personal lives. After a health crisis, one couple found the luxurious tub for two they toiled to install had become a specter of a bad slip and a potential safety risk. It's important to think through what your physical reality could be. I always emphasize to my clients that they should plan for whatever their long-term future might hold, but it's amazing how many people don't give it much thought.

## *Contracts and Regulations*

If you are looking into a cross-country move, be aware of new tax tables or local ordinances in the area where you are looking to move. After all, you don't want to experience sticker-shock when you are looking at downsizing or reducing your bills in retirement.

Along the same lines, if you are moving into a retirement community, be sure to look at the fine print. What happens if you must move into a different situation for long-term care? Will you be penalized? Will you be responsible for replacing your slot in the community? What are all the fees, and what do they cover?

# Inflation

As I write this in 2023, America has experienced a wave of inflation following a lengthy period of low inflation. Inflation zoomed to 9.1 percent in June 2022, its highest mark since November 1981.[22]

Core inflation is yet another measurement that excludes goods with prices that tend to be more volatile, such as food and energy costs. Core inflation for a 12-month period ending in December 2022 was 5.7 percent. It so happened energy prices rose 7.3 percent over that timeframe.[23]

However, inflation isn't a one-time bump; it has a cumulative effect. Again, that can impact the price of groceries greater than other goods. Even with relatively low inflation over the past few decades, an item you bought in 1997 for two dollars will cost about $3.70 today.[24] Want to go to a show? A $20 ticket in 1997 would cost $43.01 in 2023.[25]

What if, in retirement, we hit a stretch like the late seventies and early eighties, when annual inflation rates of 10 percent became the norm? It may be wise to consider some extra padding in your retirement income plan to account for any potential increase in inflation in the future.

---

[22] tradingeconomics.com. 2022 Data/2023 Forecast/1914-2021 Historical. "United States Inflation Rate" https://tradingeconomics.com/united-states/inflation-cpi

[23] U.S. Inflation Calculator. "United States Core Inflation Rates (1957-2022)" https://www.usinflationcalculator.com/inflation/united-states-core-inflation-rates/

[24] In2013dollars.com. "$2 in 1997 is worth $3.70 today" https://www.in2013dollars.com/us/inflation/1997?amount=2

[25] In2013dollars.com "Admission to movies, theaters, and concerts priced at $20 in 1997>$40.34 in 2022" https://www.in2013dollars.com/Admission-to-movies,-theaters,-and-concerts/price-inflation

## Aging

Also, in the expense category, think about longevity. We all hope to age gracefully. However, it's important to face the prospect of aging with a sense of realism.

The elephant in the room for many families is long-term care. No one wants to admit they will likely need it, but estimates indicate almost 70 percent of us will.[26] Aging is a significant piece of retirement income planning because you'll want to figure out how to set aside money for your care, either at home or away from it. The more comfortable you get with discussing your wishes and plans with your loved ones, the easier planning for the financial side of it can be.

I denote health care and potential long-term care costs in more detail elsewhere in this book, but suffice it to say nursing home care tends to be very expensive and typically isn't something you get to choose when you will need.

It isn't just the costs of long-term care that pose a concern in living longer. It's also about covering the possible costs of everything else associated with living longer. For instance, if Henry retires from his job as a biochemical engineer at age sixty-five, perhaps he planned to have a very decent income for twenty years, until age eighty-five. But what if he lives until he's ninety-five? That's a whole third—ten years—more of personal income he will need.

## Putting It All Together

Whew! So, you have pulled together what you have, and you have a pretty good idea of where you want to be. Now your financial professional and you can go about the work of arranging what assets you *have* to cover what you *need*—and how you might try to cover any gaps.

---

[26] Moll Law Group. 2022. "The Cost of Long-Term Care." https://www.molllawgroup.com/the-cost-of-long-term-care.html

Like the proverbial man in the Bible who built his house on a rock, I like to help my clients figure out how to cover their day-to-day living expenses—their needs—with insurance and other guaranteed income sources like pensions and Social Security.

Our unique planning process is called The LifeWealth Dream Builder. I'm a huge believer in dreaming. Everything significant in life starts with a dream, and DREAM is an acronym for the five steps of our process.

The D stands for the **Discovery** of the client. We take the time to fully discover the family's vision, priorities, and goals. A fun exercise they complete is creating a dream list of goals to accomplish or problems to solve in the next three years. Often couples don't have this level of deep discussion about what's most important to them, and this exercise gives them a chance to open the door to explore each other's dreams, and take the next powerful step in writing it down. I believe something magical happens when a couple has written life goals. Once written down, those goals become more real.

After we have finished the discovery phase, we look at their current **Reality:** How they are investing, what different types of investment vehicles they have been exposed to, how they manage cash flow, and how they make financial decisions.

We use our IMPACT analysis to identify opportunities to help optimize their current planning and investment strategies, looking specifically at risk, taxes, investment performance, fees, and unknown and unnecessary wealth transfers. These considerations sometimes reveal mistakes people make and can contribute to them losing money. Our IMPACT analysis enables us to quantify the difference we can make in working together.

The next phase is **Evaluating** the gap between where they are and where they want to be. We analyze the size of the gap and determine where changes could be made.

This leads us to the **Action** list of strategies and tactics to recommend bringing about the change and helping to close the gap. We evaluate the different investment platforms and insurance options we believe will work for them. We can then start educating and explaining the recommended strategies for full disclosure and understanding for our families. Then we implement the agreed-upon changes.

Our final phase is the ongoing **Monitoring** of their plan and approach. We accomplish this through our strategic and tactical meetings. We also regularly review the performance and risk of our current investment platforms, bringing about change when market circumstances dictate. We make proactive investment and financial planning recommendations to help them accomplish those dreams, which is why we call it The LifeWealth Dream Builder process. It is all designed to help see more dreams come true.

Again, you should keep in mind there isn't one single financial vehicle, asset, or source to fill all your needs, and that's okay. One of the challenges of planning for your income in retirement concerns figuring out what products and strategies to use. You can release some of that stress when you accept the fact you will probably need a diverse portfolio—potentially with bonds, stocks, insurance, and other income sources—not just one massive money pile.

One way to help shore up your income gaps is by working with your financial professional and a qualified tax advisor to help mitigate your tax exposure. If you have a 401(k) or IRA, a tax advisor in your corner may be able to help you figure out how and when to take distributions from your account in a way that doesn't push you into a higher tax bracket. Or you might learn how to use tax-advantaged bonds more effectively. Effective tax planning isn't necessarily about "adding" to your income. Especially regarding retirement, it's less about what you make than it is about what you keep. Paying a lower tax bill keeps more money in your pocket, which is where you want it when it comes to retirement income.

Now you can look at ways to cover your remaining retirement goals. Are there products like long-term care insurance specific to a certain kind of expense you anticipate? Is there a particular asset you want to use for your "play" money—money for trips and gifts for the grandkids? Is there any way you can portion off money for those charitable legacy plans?

Once you have analyzed your income wants, needs, and the assets to realistically cover them, you may have a gap. The masterstroke of a competent financial professional will be to help you figure out how you will cover that gap. Will you need to cut out a round of golf a week? Maybe skip the new car? Or will you need to take more substantial action?

One way to cover an income gap is to consider working longer or even part-time before retirement and even after that magical calendar date. This may not be the best "plan" for you; disabilities, work demands, and physical or emotional limitations can hinder the best-laid plans to continue working. However, if it is physically possible for you, this is one considerable way to help your assets last, for more than one reason.

In fact, 46 percent of the Americans responding to a survey report they plan to work part-time after retiring, while 18 percent indicated they planned to work past the age of seventy.[27]

A couple let's call them, Tom and Sue came to see us after attending one of our seminars, and I remember them being interested to know if they could retire in the next year. They both were middle to upper managers in their organizations. They were frugal and wise in accumulating and saving money for retirement.

They had a gut feeling that maybe they could afford to retire, but they wanted to be sure. They also knew they needed to figure out exactly what to plan for. After we reviewed their situation, it became evident that they could retire in the next

---

[27] Palash Ghosh. Forbes.com. May 6, 2021. "A Third Of Seniors Seek To Work Well Past Retirement Age, Or Won't Retire At All, Poll Finds" https://www.forbes.com/sites/palashghosh/2021/05/06/a-third-of-seniors-seek-to-work-well-past-retirement-age-or-wont-retire-at-all-poll-finds/?sh=1d2ece836b95

year. What was more stunning to me was the discussion about what retirement looked like for them.

The Dream Builder process covers our clients' spending plans and dream lists and opens discussions with them about what they plan to do with their lives, their time, and their wealth, as well as their talents and experiences. How will they redeploy that for the rest of their lives after they retire? We have deep and thought-provoking conversations in which we help our clients analyze their talents, areas of passion, and interests.

Tom and Sarah found opportunities to deploy their time, talent, and treasure to make a difference in people's lives and pursue causes for which they expressed passion. The result was excitement and a refiring of life's purpose.

This conversation helped them better enjoy much more adventure now, and not live in a way that they die with millions in the bank. We encourage people to plan so that you can see and experience what wealth can do for you, your family, and your community.

I believe the lack of a detailed financial plan can be one of the biggest stumbling blocks to financial freedom. Without a plan, you may lack the confidence to spend your money now, building memories and impacting your family and community. The belief that you can use your capital now and not have to hold on to all of it can be empowering.

What do you want? To die with millions and big regrets, or to have enough to still be independent but with a heart full of joy and memories of loving those closest to you? What do you take with you to the next life? Nothing, right? When you're retired, you no longer have an employer paying you a steady check. It is up to you to make sure you have saved and planned for the income you need.

CHAPTER 5

# Social Security

Social Security is often the foundation of retirement income. Backed by the strength of the U.S. Treasury, it provides perhaps the most dependable paycheck you will have in retirement.

From the time you collect your first paycheck from the job that made you a bonafide taxpayer (, you are paying into the grand old Social Security system. For me, it was selling advertising in a business directory as a self-employed contractor in Orlando, Florida, not even aware of the larger Social Security and Medicare tax I had to pay. What grew and developed out of the pressures of the Great Depression has become one of the most popular government programs in the country, and, if you pay in for the equivalent of ten years or more, you, too, can benefit from the Social Security program.

Now, before we get into the nitty-gritty of Social Security, I'd like to address a current concern: Will Social Security still be there for you when you reach retirement age?

## The Future of Social Security

This question is ever-present as headlines trumpet an underfunded Social Security program, alongside the sea of baby boomers retiring in droves and the comparatively smaller pool of younger people who are funding the system.

The Social Security Administration itself acknowledges this concern as each Social Security statement now contains a link to its website (ssa.gov) and a page entitled, "Will Social Security Be There For Me?"

Just a reminder, as if you needed one, that nothing in life is guaranteed. Additionally, depending on who you're listening to, Social Security funds may run low before 2034 thanks to the financial instability and government spending that accompanied the 2020 COVID-19 pandemic.

Before you get too discouraged, though, here are a few thoughts to keep you going:

- Even if the program is only paying 78 cents on the dollar for scheduled benefits, 78 percent is notably not zero.
- The Social Security Administration has made changes in the distant and near past to protect the fund's solvency, including increasing retirement ages and striking certain filing strategies.
- There are many changes Congress could make, and lawmakers routinely discuss how to fix the system, such as further increasing full retirement age and eligibility.
- One thing no one is seriously discussing? Reneging on current obligations to retirees or the soon-to-retire.

Take heart. The real answer to the question, "Will Social Security be there for me?" is still yes.

This question is important to consider when you look at how much we, as a nation, rely on this program. Did you know Social Security benefits replace about 40 percent of a person's original income when they retire?[28]

If you ask me, that's a pretty significant piece of your retirement income puzzle.

---

[28] ssa.gov. "Alternate Measure of Replacement Rates for Social Security Benefits and Retirement Income" https://www.ssa.gov/policy/docs/ssb/v68n2/v68n2p1.html.

Another caveat? You may not realize this, but no one can legally "advise" you about your Social Security benefits.

"But, Hilgardt," you may be thinking, "isn't that part of what you do? And what about that nice gentleman at the Social Security Administration office I spoke with on the phone?"

Don't get me wrong. Social Security Administration employees know their stuff. They are trained to understand policies and programs, and they are usually pretty quick to tell you what you can and cannot do. But the government specifically stipulates, because Social Security is a benefit you alone have paid into and earned, your Social Security decisions, too, are yours alone.

When it comes to financial professionals, we can't push you in any direction, but—there's a big but here—working with a well-informed financial professional is still incredibly handy for your Social Security decisions. Why? Because someone who's worth his or her salt will know what withdrawal strategies might pertain to your specific situation and will ask questions that can help you determine what you are looking for when it comes to your Social Security.

For instance, some people want the highest possible monthly benefit. Others want to start their benefits early, not always because of financial need. I heard about one man who called in to start his Social Security payments the day he qualified, just because he liked to think of it as the government paying back a debt it owed him, and he enjoyed the feeling of receiving a check from Uncle Sam.

Whatever your reasons, questions, or feelings regarding Social Security, the decision is yours alone; but working with a financial professional can help you put your options in perspective by showing you—both with industry knowledge and with proprietary software or planning processes— where your benefits fit into your overall strategy for retirement income.

One reason the federal government doesn't allow for "advice" related to Social Security, I suspect, is so no one can profit from giving you advice related to your Social Security benefit—or from providing any clarifications. Again, this is a sign of an experienced financial professional. Those who are passionate about their work will be knowledgeable about what benefit strategies might be to your advantage and will happily share those possible options with you.

# Full Retirement Age

When it comes to Social Security, it seems like many people only think so far as "yes." They don't take the time to understand the various options available. Instead, because it is common knowledge you can begin your benefits at age sixty-two, that's what many of us do. While more people are opting to delay taking benefits, age sixty-two is still firmly the most popular age to start.[29]

What many people fail to understand is, by starting benefits early, they may be leaving a lot of money on the table. You see, the Social Security Administration bases your monthly benefit on two factors: your earnings history and your full retirement age (FRA).

From your earnings history, they pull the thirty-five years you made the most money and use a mathematical indexing formula to figure out a monthly average from those years. If you paid into the system for less than thirty-five years, then every year you didn't pay in will be counted as a zero.

Once they have calculated what your monthly earning would be at FRA, the government then calculates what to put on your check based on how close you are to FRA. FRA was originally set at sixty-five, but, as the population aged and lifespans lengthened, the government shifted FRA later and later, based

---

[29] Chris Kissell. moneytalknews.com. January 20, 2021. "This Is When the Most People Start Taking Social Security."
https://www.moneytalksnews.com/the-most-popular-age-for-claiming-social-security/

on an individual's year of birth. Check out the following chart to see when you will reach FRA.[30]

---

[30] Social Security Administration. "Full Retirement Age." https://www.ssa.gov/planners/retire/retirechart.html

| Age to Receive Full Social Security Benefits* ||
|---|---|
| *(Called "full retirement age" [FRA] or "normal retirement age.")* ||
| Year of Birth* | FRA |
| 1937 or earlier | 65 |
| 1938 | 65 and 2 months |
| 1939 | 65 and 4 months |
| 1940 | 65 and 6 months |
| 1941 | 65 and 8 months |
| 1942 | 65 and 10 months |
| 1943-1954 | 66 |
| 1955 | 66 and 2 months |
| 1956 | 66 and 4 months |
| 1957 | 66 and 6 months |
| 1958 | 66 and 8 months |
| 1959 | 66 and 10 months |
| 1960 and later | 67 |
| *If you were born on Jan. 1 of any year, you should refer to the previous year. (If you were born on the 1st of the month, we figure your benefit [and your full retirement age] as if your birthday was in the previous month.)* ||

When you reach FRA, you are eligible to receive 100 percent of whatever the Social Security Administration says is your full monthly benefit.

Starting at age sixty-two, for every year before FRA you claim benefits, your monthly check is reduced by 5 percent or more. Conversely, for every year you delay taking benefits past FRA, your monthly benefit increases by 8 percent (until age seventy—after that, there is no monetary advantage to delaying Social Security benefits). While your circumstances and needs may vary, a lot of financial professionals still urge people to at least consider delaying until they reach age seventy.

Why wait?[31]

| Taking benefits early could affect your monthly check by ____. |||||||||
|---|---|---|---|---|---|---|---|---|
| 62 | 63 | 64 | 65 | FRA 66 | 67 | 68 | 69 | 70 |
| -25% | -20% | -13.3% | -6.7% | 0 | +8% | +16% | +24% | +32% |

## My Social Security

If you are over age thirty, you have probably received a notice from the Social Security Administration telling you to activate something called "My Social Security." This is a handy way to learn more about your particular benefit options, to keep track of what your earnings record looks like, and to calculate the benefits you have accrued over the years.

Essentially, My Social Security is an online account you can activate to see what your personal Social Security picture looks like, which you can do at www.ssa.gov/myaccount. This can be extremely helpful when it comes to planning for income in retirement and figuring up the difference between your anticipated income versus anticipated expenses.

---

[31] Social Security Administration. April 2021. "Can You Take Your Benefits Before Full Retirement Age?" https://www.ssa.gov/planners/retire/applying2.html

## COLA

Social Security is a largely guaranteed piece of the retirement puzzle: If you get a statement that reads you should expect $1,000 a month, you can be sure you will receive $1,000 a month. But there is one variable detail, and that is something called the cost-of-living adjustment, or COLA.

The COLA is an increase in your monthly check meant to address inflation in everyday life. After all, your expenses will likely continue to experience inflation in retirement, but you will no longer have the opportunity for raises, bonuses, or promotions you had when you were working. Instead, Social Security receives an annual cost-of-living increase tied to the Department of Labor's Consumer Price Index for Urban Wage Earners and Clerical Workers, or CPI-W. If the CPI-W measurement shows inflation rose a certain amount for regular goods and services, then Social Security recipients will see that reflected in their COLA.

COLA adjustments have climbed as high as 14.3 percent (1980) and in 2023 reached 8.7 percent, the largest increase in more than forty years. But in a no- or low-inflation environment, such as in 2010, 2011, and 2016, Social Security recipients will not receive an adjustment.[32] Some view the COLA as a perk, bump, or bonus, but, in reality, it works more like this: Your mom sends you to the store with $2.50 for a gallon of milk. Milk costs exactly $2.50. The next week, you go back with that same amount, but it is now $2.52 for a gallon, so you go back to Mom, and she gives you 2 cents. You aren't bringing home more milk—it just costs more money.

So the COLA is less about "making more money" and more about keeping seniors' purchasing power from eroding when inflation is a big factor, such as in 1975, when it was 8 percent![33] Still, don't let that detract from your enthusiasm about COLAs;

---

[32] ssa.gov. "Cost-Of-Living Adjustments" ssa.gov/oact/cola/colaseries.html
[33] Social Security Administration. "Cost-Of-Living Adjustment (COLA) Information for 2022." https://www.ssa.gov/cola/

after all, what if Mom's solution was: "Here's the same $2.50; try to find pennies from somewhere else to get that milk!"?

## Spousal Benefits

We've talked about FRA, but another big Social Security decision involves spousal benefits.

If you or your spouse has a long stretch of zeros in your earnings history—perhaps if one of you stayed home for years, caring for children or sick relatives—you may want to consider filing for spousal benefits instead of filing on your own earnings history. A spousal benefit can be up to 50 percent of the primary wage earner's benefit at full retirement age.

To begin drawing a spousal benefit, you must be at least sixty-two years old, and the primary wage earner must have already filed for his or her benefit. While there are penalties for taking spousal benefits early, you cannot earn credits for delaying past full retirement age.[34]

Like I wrote, the spousal benefit can be a big deal for those who don't have a very long pay history, but it's important to weigh your own earned benefits against the option of withdrawing based on a fraction of your spouse's benefits.

To look at how this could play out, let's use a hypothetical couple: Mary Jane, who is sixty, and Peter, who is sixty-two.

Let's say Peter's benefit at FRA, in his case sixty-six, would be $1,600. If Peter begins his benefits right now, four years before FRA, his monthly check will be $1,200. If Mary Jane begins taking spousal benefits in two years at the earliest date possible, her monthly benefits will be reduced by 67.5 percent, to $520 per month (remember, at FRA, the most she can qualify for is half of Peter's FRA benefit).

What if Peter and Mary Jane both wait until FRA? At sixty-seven, Peter begins taking his full benefit of $1,600 a month. Two years later, when she reaches age sixty-seven, Mary Jane

---

[34] Social Security Administration. "Retirement Planner: Benefits For You As A Spouse." https://www.ssa.gov/planners/retire/applying6.html

will qualify for $800 a month. By waiting until FRA, the couple's monthly benefit goes from $1,720 to $2,400.

What if Peter delays until age seventy to get his maximum possible benefit? For each year past FRA he delays, his monthly benefits increase by 8 percent. This means, at seventy, he could file for a monthly benefit of $2,015. However, delayed retirement credits do not affect spousal benefits, so as soon as Peter files at seventy, Mary Jane would also file (at age sixty-eight) for her maximum benefit of $800, so their highest possible combined monthly check is $2,815.[35]

When it comes to your Social Security benefits, you obviously will want to consider whether a monthly check based on a fraction of your spouse's earnings will be comparable to or larger than your own earnings history.

## Divorced Spouses

There are a few considerations for those of us who have gone through a divorce. If you 1) were married for ten years or more *and* 2) have since been divorced for at least two years *and* 3) are unmarried *and* 4) your ex-spouse qualifies to begin Social Security, you qualify for a spousal benefit based on your ex-husband or ex-wife's earnings history at FRA. A divorced spousal benefit is different from the married spousal benefit in one way: You don't have to wait for your ex-spouse to file before you can file yourself.[36]

For instance, Charles and Moira were married for fifteen years before their divorce, when he was thirty-six and she was forty. Moira has been remarried for twenty years, and, although Charles briefly remarried, his second marriage ended after a few years. Charles' benefits are largely calculated based on his

---

[35] Office of the Chief Actuary. Social Security Administration. "Social Security Benefits: Benefits for Spouses." https://www.ssa.gov/OACT/quickcalc/spouse.html#calculator

[36] Social Security Administration. "Retirement Planner: If You Are Divorced." https://www.ssa.gov/planners/retire/divspouse.html

many years of volunteering in schools, meaning his personal monthly benefit is close to zero.

Although Moira has deferred her retirement, opting to delay benefits until she is seventy, Charles can begin taking benefits calculated from Moira's work history at FRA as early as sixty-two. However, he will also have the option of waiting until FRA to collect the maximum, or 50 percent of Moira's earned monthly benefit at her FRA.

## Widowed Spouses

If your marriage ended with the death of your spouse, you might claim a benefit for your spouse's earned income as his or her widow/widower, called a survivor's benefit. Unlike a spousal benefit or divorced benefits, if your husband or wife dies, you can claim his or her full benefit. Also, unlike spousal benefits, if you need to, you can begin taking income when you turn sixty. However, as with other benefit options, your monthly check will be permanently reduced for withdrawing benefits before FRA.

If your spouse began taking benefits before he or she died, you can't delay withdrawing your survivor's benefits to get delayed credits. The Social Security Administration maintains you can only get as much from a survivor's benefit as your deceased spouse might have received, had he or she lived.[37]

# Taxes, Taxes, Taxes

With Social Security, as with everything, it is important to consider taxes. It may be surprising, but your Social Security benefits are not tax-free. Despite having been taxed to accrue those benefits in the first place, you may have to pay Uncle Sam income taxes on up to 85 percent of your Social Security.

---

[37] Social Security Administration. "Social Security Benefit Amounts For The Surviving Spouse By Year Of Birth."
https://www.ssa.gov/planners/survivors/survivorchartred.html

The Social Security Administration figures these taxes using what they call "the provisional income formula." Your provisional income formula differs from the adjusted gross income you use for your regular income taxes. Instead, to find out how much of your Social Security benefit is taxable, the Social Security Administration calculates it this way:

*Provisional Income = Adjusted Gross Income + Nontaxable Interest + ½ of Social Security*

See that piece about nontaxable interest? That generally means interest from government bonds and notes. It surprises many people that, although you may not pay taxes on those assets, their income will count against you when it comes to Social Security taxation.

Once you have figured out your provisional income (also called "combined income"), you can use the following chart to figure out your Social Security taxes.[38]

---

[38] Social Security Administration. "Benefits Planner: Income Taxes and Your Social Security Benefits." https://www.ssa.gov/planners/taxes.html

| Taxes on Social Security | | |
|---|---|---|
| *Provisional Income = Adjusted Gross Income + Nontaxable Interest + ½ of Social Security* | | |
| If you are ___ and your provisional income is ___, then . . . | | Uncle Sam will tax ___ of your Social Security |
| Single | Married, filing jointly | |
| Less than $25,000 | Less than $32,000 | 0% |
| $25,000 to $34,000 | $32,000 to $44,000 | Up to 50% |
| More than $34,000 | More than $44,000 | Up to 85% |

This is one more reason it may benefit you to work with financial and tax professionals. They can help you look at your entire financial picture to make your overall retirement plan as tax-efficient as possible—including your Social Security benefit. Interest income, dividends, and capital gains from investments add to this provisional income calculation. So, the investments you have are hurting you in the calculation of taxation of your Social Security benefit. This may be a good opportunity to establish a detailed income plan for the rest of your life and evaluate your income needs in the near term. Now we can look at possibly moving taxable interest to tax-deferred or tax-free areas. This income can be delayed until you need it and still be earned but without aggravating the current provisional income calculations.

# Working and Social Security: The Earnings Test

If you haven't reached FRA, but you started your Social Security benefits and are still working, things get a little hairy.

Because you have started Social Security payments, the Social Security Administration will pay out your benefits (at that reduced rate, of course, because you haven't reached your FRA). Yet, because you are working, the organization must also withhold from your check to add to your benefits, which you are already collecting. See how this complicates matters?

To address the situation, the government has what is called the earnings test. For 2023, you can earn up to $21,240 without it affecting your Social Security check if you're younger than full retirement age. But, for every $2 you earn past that amount, the Social Security Administration will withhold $1. The earnings test loosens in the year of your FRA; if you are reaching FRA in 2023, you can earn up to $56,520 before you run into the earnings test, and the government only withholds $1 for every $3 past that amount.

The month you reach FRA, you are no longer subject to any earnings withholding. For instance, if you are still working and will turn sixty-six on December 28, 2023, you would only have to worry about the earnings test until December, and then you can ignore it entirely. Keep in mind, the money the government withholds from your Social Security benefits while you are working before FRA will be tacked back onto your benefits check after FRA.[39]

Most of the families we work with state that they have paid into the Social Security system for a long time and want to optimize what they receive from the system. We agree. Optimizing Social Security typically requires detailed planning. Following The LifeWealth Dream Builder process gives us the

---

[39] Social Security Administration. "Receiving Benefits White Working" https://www.ssa.gov/benefits/retirement/planner/whileworking.html.

information needed to evaluate every aspect to work towards optimization.

We look at cash flow desire as the first factor. Many of our families today don't retire with zero income. They step down from their work responsibilities and move to semi-retired and then a full retirement. This helps allow many families to avoid the reduction of Social Security due to earning income since the part-time income could still be sufficient for the family's needs.

Another area to consider is the assets of a family. The earlier you take Social Security, the more compounding you are affording your assets. Often, this could be a larger benefit than avoiding taxation or even a reduction of income from Social Security. Another factor is the amount of permanent life insurance a husband and wife have. This is a factor in the survival benefit for a single remaining spouse.

We ultimately want to plan to optimize LifeWealth for both spouses and the remaining spouse at the first death.

Planning can help with the optimization of Social Security. The same applies when planning how to receive a pension from work. Most people qualify for their pension based on how much they have paid in during their working years.

CHAPTER 6

# 401(k)s & IRAs

Have you heard? Today's retirement is not your parents' retirement. You see, back in the day, it was pretty common to work for one company for the vast majority of your career and then retire with a gold watch and a pension.

The gold watch was a symbol of the quality time you had put in at that company, but the pension was more than a symbol. Instead, it was a guarantee—as solid as your employer—that they would repay your hard work with a certain amount of income in your old age. Did you see the caveat there? Your pension's guarantee was *as solid as your employer*. The problem was, what if your employer went under?

Companies that failed couldn't pay their retired employees' pensions, leading to financial challenges for many. Beginning in 1974 with Congress' passage of the Employee Retirement Income Security Act, federal legislation and regulations aimed at protecting retirees were everywhere. One piece of legislation included a relatively obscure section of the Internal Revenue Code, added in 1978. Section 401(k), to be specific.

IRC section 401, subsection k, created tax advantages for employer-sponsored financial products, even if the main contributor was the employee him or herself. Over the years, more employers took note, beginning an age of transition away from pensions and toward 401(k) plans. A 401(k) is a retirement account with certain tax benefits and restrictions on the investments or other financial products inside of it.

Essentially, 401(k)s and their individual retirement account (IRA) counterparts are "wrappers" that provide tax benefits around assets; typically, the assets that compose IRAs and 401(k)s are mutual funds, stock and bond mixes, and money market accounts. However, IRA and 401(k) contents are becoming more diverse these days, with some companies offering different kinds of annuity options within their plans.

Where pensions are defined-*benefit* plans, 401(k)s and IRAs are defined-*contribution* plans. The one-word change outlines the basic difference. Pensions spell out what you can expect to receive from the plan but not necessarily how much money it will take to fund those benefits. With 401(k)s, an employer sets a standard for how much they will contribute (if any), and you can be certain of what you are contributing. Still, there is no outline for what you can expect to receive in return for those contributions.

Modern employment looks very different. A 2020 survey by the Bureau of Labor Statistics determined U.S. workers stayed with their employers a median of 4.1 years. Workers ages fifty-five to sixty-four had a little more staying power and were most likely to stay with their employer for about ten years.[40] Participation in 401(k) plans has steadily risen this century, totaling $7.3 trillion in assets in 2021 compared to $3.1 trillion in 2011. About 60 million active participants engaged in 401(k) plans in 2020.[41]

Those statistics make it clear that 401(k) plans have replaced pensions at many companies and, for that matter, a gold watch.

---

[40] Bureau of Labor Statistics. September 22, 2022. "Employee Tenure Summary." https://www.bls.gov/news.release/tenure.nr0.htm
[41] Investment Company Institute. October 11, 2021. "Frequently Asked Questions About 401(k) Plan Research" https://www.ici.org/faqs/faq/401k/faqs_401k#:~:text=In%202020%2C%20there%20were%20about,of%20former%20employees%20and%20retirees.

We still work with many families that are fortunate enough to have pensions. Most families recognize the benefit of their pension, but they don't always know exactly how good of a deal this can be. How a couple should decide to take their pension is a big opportunity for planning to optimize this decision. Similar to the decision of Social Security, they have to determine when and in what way they choose to receive their benefit. It can be complicated since most employers offer more than one choice to receive the benefit, and you should consider the lives of two spouses.

Our strategy? You guessed it—The LifeWealth Dream Builder process. Here again, we can isolate this decision in the luxury of having the full context of the plan. The results for many families could be significant since there may be large differences in the total benefit from the different choices.

When working with pensions, we first analyze the pension and Social Security together and then examine the appropriate spend-down plan for the assets. Next, we look at the right tax and investment strategies for the different types of accounts. It can get complicated, especially if you are evaluating whether Roth conversions make sense in the middle of all this planning.

The LifeWealth Dream Builder process enables us to pull the different layers of the" onion of factors" apart one layer at a time, then put it back together in the correct sequence to help optimize the total picture. If there is anything to learn from this paradigm shift, it's that you must look out for yourself. Whether you have worked for a company for two years or twenty, you still have to look out for your best interests. That holds doubly true when it comes to preparing for retirement. If you are one of the lucky ones who still has a pension, good for you. But for the rest of us, it is likely a 401(k)—or possibly one of its nonprofit, or government-sector counterparts, a 403(b) or 457 plan—is one of your biggest assets for retirement.

Some employers offer incentives to contribute to their company plans, like a company match. On that subject, I have one thing to say: *Do it!* Nothing in life is free, as they say, but a company match on your retirement funds is about as close to free money as it gets. If you can make the minimum to qualify for your company's match at all, go for it.

Now, it's likely, during our working years, we mostly "set and forget" our 401(k) funding. Because it is tax-advantaged, your employer is taking money from your paycheck—before taxes—and putting it into your plan for you. Maybe you got to pick a selection of investments, or maybe your company only offers one choice of investment in your 401(k). Either way, while you are gainfully employed, your most impactful decision may just be the decision to continue funding your plan in the first place. But, when you are ready to retire or move jobs, you have choices to make requiring a little more thought and care.

When you are ready to part ways with your job, you have a few options:
- Leave the money where it is
- Take the cash (and pay income taxes and perhaps a 10 percent additional federal tax if you are younger than age fifty-nine-and-one-half)
- Transfer the money to another employer plan (if the new plan allows)
- Roll the money over into a self-directed IRA

Now, these are just general options. You will have to decide, hopefully with the help of a financial professional, what's right for you. For instance, 401(k)s are typically pretty closely tied to the companies offering them, so when changing jobs, it may not always be possible to transfer a 401(k) to another 401(k). Leaving the money where it is may also be out of the question—some companies have direct cash payout or rollover policies once someone is no longer employed.

Also, remember what we mentioned earlier about how we change jobs more often these days? That means you likely have a 401(k) with your current company, but you may also have a string of retirement accounts trailing you from other jobs.

When we start working with a new family, we gather all their account information. For our families, it can feel eye opening.

They "find" money they forgot about—like jeans coming out of the wash, and a very "clean" twenty-dollar bill is in the pocket.

We enjoy celebrating the moment with them, but then reality sets in. How is that money invested, and how long has it been sitting there? Who is paying attention to the investment allocation? Who's managing it? The room gets quiet, normally, and the answer is often "my old employer's investment company." Why can this be a big deal?

I have to bring up the enthusiasm in the room again and explain, "You have a sleeping giant here." Then they ask, "What do you mean, Hilgardt?" I explain that 90 percent of an account's ultimate value at retirement has to do with the asset allocation strategy that was followed, whether forgotten and just riding along the stormy waves of the open economy or carefully planned and assessed, navigated to move through the storms of life and the economy. We talk about compound interest and the difference a 1 percent average growth rate makes over time on a balance equal to the total of all the old 401(k) accounts. It is typically a substantial difference.

Then the excitement escalates again when we discuss consolidating the accounts and applying a unique asset management style that can possibly make a positive impact on their account.

There also is a cost difference to consider in leaving the 401(k) plans where they are or consolidating them. We analyze this as well to determine the ideal cause of action. The ultimate goal is to succeed and optimize.

When it comes to your retirement income, it's important to be able to pull together *all* your assets, so you can examine what you have and where, and then decide what you will do with it.

## Tax-Qualified, Tax-Preferred, Tax-Deferred ... Still TAXED

Financial media often cite IRAs and 401(k)s for their tax benefits. After all, with traditional plans, you put your money in, pre-tax, and it hopefully grows for years, even decades, untaxed. That's why these accounts are called "tax-qualified" or "tax-deferred" assets. They aren't *tax-free!* Rarely does Uncle Sam allow business to continue without receiving his piece of the pie, and your retirement assets are no different. If you didn't pay taxes on the front end, you will pay taxes on the money you withdraw from these accounts in retirement. Don't get me wrong: This isn't an inherently good or bad thing; it's just the way it is. It's important to understand, though, for the sake of planning ahead.

In retirement, many people assume they will be in a lower tax bracket. Are you planning to pare down your lifestyle in retirement? Perhaps you are, and perhaps you will have substantially less income in retirement. But many of my clients tell me they want to live life more or less the same as they always have. The money they would previously have spent on business attire or gas for their commute they now want to spend on hobbies and grandchildren. That's all fine, and for many of them, it is doable, but does it put them in a lower tax bracket? Probably not.

Keep in mind, IRAs, 401(k)s, and their alternatives have a few limitations because of their special tax status. For one thing, the IRS sets limits on your contributions to these retirement accounts. If you are contributing to a 401(k) or an equivalent nonprofit or government plan, your annual contribution limit is $22,500 (as of 2023). If you are fifty or older, the IRS allows additional contributions, called "catch-up contributions," of up to $7,500 on top of the regular limit of $22,500. For an IRA, the limit is $6,500, with a catch-up limit of an additional $1,000.[42] Beginning in 2024, catch-up contributions for individuals with income exceeding $145,000 must transfer into a Roth IRA.[43]

---

[42] IRS.gov. December 8, 2022. "401(k) limit increases to $22,500 for 2023, IRA limit rises to $6,500" https://www.irs.gov/newsroom/401k-limit-increases-to-22500-for-2023-ira-limit-rises-to-6500

[43] Fidelity.com. 2023. "SECURE 2.0: Rethinking retirement savings" https://www.fidelity.com/learning-center/personal-finance/secure-act-2

Because their tax advantages come from their intended use as retirement income, withdrawing funds from these accounts before you turn fifty-nine-and-one-half can carry stiff penalties. In addition to fees your investment management company might charge, you will have to pay income tax *and* a 10 percent federal tax penalty, with few exceptions.

The fifty-nine-and-one-half rule for retirement accounts is incredibly important to remember, especially when you're young. Younger workers are often tempted to cash out an IRA from a previous employer and then are surprised to find their checks missing 20 percent of the account value to income taxes, penalty taxes, and account fees.

Many millennials I see in my practice say, while they may be socking money away in their workplace retirement plan, it is often the *only* place they are saving. This could be problematic later because of the fifty-nine-and-one-half rule; what if you have an emergency? It is important to fund your retirement, but you need to have some liquid assets handy as emergency funds. This can help you avoid breaking into your retirement accounts and incurring taxes and penalties because of the fifty-nine-and-one-half rule.

## RMDs

Remember how we talked about the 401(k) or IRA being a "tax wrapper" for your funds? Well, eventually, Uncle Sam will want a bite of that candy bar. So, when you turn seventy-two, the government requires you withdraw a portion of your account, which the IRS calculates based on the size of your account and your estimated lifespan. This required minimum distribution, or RMD, is the government's insurance it will collect some taxes, at some point, from your earnings. Because you didn't pay taxes on the front end, you will now pay income taxes on whatever you withdraw, including your RMDs.

Let me reiterate something I pointed out in the Longevity chapter. Beginning at age seventy-three, you are required to withdraw a certain minimum amount every year from your 401(k) or IRA, or else you will face a tax penalty on any RMD monies you should have withdrawn but didn't—and that's on top of income tax. The SECURE Act 2.0 reduced the penalty to 25 percent (from 50 percent). Timely corrections also can reduce the penalty to 10 percent.[44]

Even after you begin RMDs, you can still also continue contributing to your 401(k) or IRAs if you are still employed, which can affect the whole discussion on RMDs and possible tax considerations. The SECURE Act 2.0 raised the RMD age to seventy-three from seventy-two. In addition, the latest legislation stipulates the RMD age will increase to seventy-five for those turning seventy-four after December 31, 2032.[45]

If you don't need income from your retirement accounts, RMDs can seem like more of a tax burden than an income boon. While some people prefer to reinvest their RMDs, this comes with the possibility of additional taxation: You'll pay income taxes on your RMDs and then potential capital gains taxes on the growth of your investments. If you are legacy-minded, there are other ways to use RMDs, many of which have tax benefits.

## *SECURE Act 2.0 provisions*

In addition to changes imposed for RMD ages, Secure Act 2.0 also expanded access to retirement savings using different methods. Provisions in the legislation go into effect at different times, ranging from 2023-25.

- Beginning January 2, 2024, plan participants can access up to $1,000 (once a year) from retirement savings for emergency personal or family expenses without paying a 10 percent early withdrawal penalty.
- Beginning January 2, 2024, employees can establish a Roth emergency savings account of up to $2,500 per participant.

---

[44] Jim Probasco. Investopedia.com. January 6, 2023. "SECURE 2.0 Act of 2022." https://www.investopedia.com/secure-2-0-definition-5225115
[45] Ibid.

- Beginning January 2, 2024, domestic abuse survivors can withdraw the lesser of $10,000 or 50 percent of their retirement account without penalty.
- Beginning January 1, 2023, victims of a qualified, federally declared disaster can withdraw up to $22,000 from their retirement account without penalty.[46]

### *Permanent Life Insurance*

One way to turn those pesky RMDs into a legacy is through permanent life insurance. Assuming you need the death benefit coverage and can qualify for it medically, if properly structured, these products can pass on a sizeable death benefit to your beneficiaries, tax-free, as part of your general legacy plan.

### *ILIT*

Another way to use RMDs toward your legacy is to work with an estate planning attorney to create an irrevocable life insurance trust (ILIT). This is basically a permanent life insurance policy placed within a trust. Because the trust is irrevocable, you would relinquish control of it, but, unlike with just a permanent life insurance policy, your death benefit won't count toward your taxable estate.

### *Annuities*

Because annuities can be tax-deferred, using all or a portion of your RMDs to fund an annuity contract can be one way to further delay taxation while guaranteeing your income payments (either to you or your loved ones) later. Of course, this assumes you don't need the RMD income during your retirement.)

---

[46] Betterment.com. January 12, 2023. "SECURE Act 2.0: Signed into Law" https://www.betterment.com/work/resources/secure-act-2

## *Qualified Charitable Distributions*

If you are charity-minded, you may use your RMDs toward a charitable organization instead of using them for income. You must do this directly from your retirement account (you can't take the RMD check and *then* pay the charity) for your withdrawals to be qualified charitable distributions (QCDs), but this is one way of realizing some of the benefits of a charitable legacy during your own lifetime. You will not need to pay taxes on your QCDs, and they won't count toward your annual charitable tax deduction limit, plus you'll be able to see how the organization you are supporting uses your donations. You should consult a financial professional on how to correctly make a QCD.

This conversation normally evokes a lot of emotion. Many families are unaware of the amount of taxes that will be due on IRA and 401(k) accounts during the lifetimes of both spouses *and* the income tax due to their children when they inherit the funds.

A strategy we have deployed is starting the conversation with estate planning and then working back to the ideal retirement plan, as well as the family and community impact plan. When the conversation begins with comprehensive planning first, all the strategies can be used to help minimize taxes for the family.

What I am saying is that if you try to reduce taxes without looking at the big picture, you might only reduce a portion of the taxes, or you may only be putting a Band-Aid on a bullet hole.

Let me share a hypothetical example of how this can work. The Webb family meets with a financial planner. After looking at their retirement plan, they discuss how they want to leave their estate and how they would like to give during their lifetime. This conversation reveals that the Webbs won't need their IRAs during their lifetimes, so they can focus more on sufficing their RMDs with QCDs from their IRAs. Additionally, they can choose to leave the remainder of the IRA account to the family foundation account for community impact.

In utilizing these strategies, the family can make a bigger difference through charitable giving during their lives, potentially avoid all the income tax from the RMDs and overall IRAs at death, and lastly, help reduce the estate tax. They can then focus on assets going to the children that will get a step-up in cost basis at death and help eliminate income and capital taxes through inheritance completely. Their financial and tax advisors can help them evaluate if advanced strategies like charitable remainder trusts make sense to help reduce or avoid capital gains for the family, create large income tax deductions, and leave assets determined to go to the family foundation account in any way. These are just a few of the many more similar strategies available in the tax code.

This is one of my favorite areas of planning, since knowing the big picture of a family's vision, priorities, and goals can unlock many more advantageous opportunities.

## Roth IRA

Since the Taxpayer Relief Act of 1997, there has been a different kind of retirement account, or "tax wrapper," available to the public: the Roth. Roth IRAs and Roth 401(k)s each differ from their traditional counterparts in one big way: You pay your taxes on the front end. This means, once your post-tax money is in the Roth account, as long as you follow the rules and limitations of that account, your distributions are truly tax-free. You won't pay income tax when you take withdrawals, so, in turn, you don't have to worry about RMDs.

However, Roth accounts have the same limitations as traditional 401(k)s and IRAs when it comes to withdrawing money before age fifty-nine-and-one-half, with the added stipulation that the account must have been open for at least five years in order for the account holder to make withdrawals.

We often evaluate if a Roth conversion makes sense. I will start by saying it can be a great idea, but it does not make sense for everyone. It really is a custom strategy since everyone's plan is different. I would also not be able to evaluate if it makes sense without a comprehensive plan; it would be mere speculation at that point.

Much of the Roth conversion decision has to do with the issue of current versus future tax rates. Many people believe the tax rate in their working years will be higher than in retirement. I have found some CPAs believe this as well. Is it true? Maybe for some, but not for everyone.

Where did this idea come from? It gained popularity around the birth of the 401(k) plan, which originated in the late 1970s—also a time when the highest tax rate in the US was 70 percent.[47] For families to believe their tax rate in their working years (as high as 70 percent) would be lower in their retirement years was not an unreasonable assumption.

But where are we now? In 2023, the highest rate is 37 percent, and our country's debt level is at an all-time high. Where do you think the rates are heading? I'll leave that for you to decide. An often overlooked factor is the concept of compounding wealth in a tax-deferred environment versus a tax-free environment. This normally, over a period of time, can make a substantial difference. When evaluating Roth conversions, there is a multitude of factors to consider.

We start by assessing if the RMDs in the future, by their sheer size, could potentially push a family into a higher tax bracket and, therefore, put them out of control of their joint tax rate. If so, we have higher urgency in evaluating the Roth conversion. We then calculate the total tax liability of those qualified accounts over a lifetime, including the taxes that will be due from the family's heirs, so that we understand the possible severity of the issue.

Next, we use the information from the family to create a current tax return projection to show them just how their different sources of income are adding to their ultimate tax

---

[47] Tax-brackets.org. "Federal Income Tax Brackets (Tax Year 1978)" https://www.tax-brackets.org/federaltaxtable/1978

liability. We then very carefully show various scenarios designed to help reduce the total tax for them and their heirs.

So why does this not make sense for everyone? Well, when you convert, the taxable income substantially increases unless you have strategies to create large income tax deductions in the same year. We can explain those strategies. Another potential pitfall to consider is that when you convert to a Roth, you could create a much larger Medicare copayment for at least the next three years.

Any conversion should be evaluated against the possible income tax savings in the future. The final factor is: Where will the money come from to pay the additional taxes due, and what is the impact on the compounding of these assets in the future? All these factors and opposing results might make your head spin. This is why we believe you should have a comprehensive plan because, in our experience, this decision could be one of your biggest tax reduction strategies.

# Taking Charge

As mentioned earlier, the 401(k) and IRA have largely replaced pensions, but they aren't an equal trade.

Pensions are employer-funded; the money feeding into them is money that wouldn't ever show up on your pay stub. Because 401(k)s are self-funded, you must actively and consciously save. This distinction has made a difference when it comes to funding retirement. Fidelity Investments published a story detailing that the average 401(k) balance for a person age fifty-five to sixty-four is $189,800, but the median likely tells the full story. The median 401(k) balance for a person age fifty-five to sixty-four is $56,450. Those figures reflect Fidelity accounts from the third quarter of 2022.[48]

---

[48] Arielle O'Shea. Nerd Wallet. December 22, 2022. "The Average 401(k) Balance by Age" https://www.nerdwallet.com/article/investing/the-average-401k-balance-by-age

There can be many reasons why people underfund their retirement plans, like being overwhelmed by the investment choices or taking withdrawals from IRAs when they leave an employer. Still, the reason at the top of the list seems to be this: People simply aren't participating to begin with.

So, whether you use a 401(k) with an employer or an IRA alternative with a private company, separate from your workplace, the most important retirement savings decision you can make is to sock away your money somewhere in the first place.

CHAPTER 7

# Annuities

In my practice, I offer my clients a variety of products—from securities to insurance—all designed to help them work toward their financial goals. You may be wondering: Why single out a single product in this book?

Well, while most of my clients have a pretty good understanding of business and finance, I sometimes find those who have the impression there must be magic involved. Some people assume there is a magic finance wand we can wave to change years' worth of savings into a strategy for retirement income. But it's not as easy as a goose laying golden eggs or the Fairy Godmother turning a pumpkin into a coach!

Finances aren't magic; it takes lots of hard work and, typically, several financial products and strategies to pull together a complete retirement plan. Of all the financial products I work with, it seems people find none more mysterious than annuities. And, if I may say, even some of those who recognize the word "annuity" have a limited understanding of the product. So, in the interest of demystifying annuities, let me tell you a little about what an annuity is.

In general, insurance is a financial hedge against risk. Car owners buy auto insurance to protect their finances in case they injure someone or someone injures them. Homeowners have house insurance to protect their finances in case of a fire, flood, or another disaster. People have life insurance to protect their finances in case of untimely death. Almost juxtaposed to life insurance, people have annuities in case of a long life; annuities can give you financial protection by providing consistent and reliable income payments.

The basic premise of an annuity is you, the annuitant, pay an insurance company some amount in exchange for their contractual guarantee they will pay you income for a certain time period. How that company pays you, for how long, and how much they offer are all determined by the annuity contract you enter into with the insurance company.

## How You Get Paid

There are two ways for an annuity contract to provide income: The first is through what is called annuitization, and the second is through the use of income riders. We'll get into income riders in a bit, but let's talk about annuitization. That nice, long word is, in my opinion, one reason annuities have a reputation for mystery and misinformation.

## Annuitization

When someone "annuitizes" a contract, it is the point where he or she turns on the income stream. Once a contract has been annuitized, there is no going back. With annuities, if the policyholder lives longer than the insurance company planned, the insurance company is still obligated to pay him or her, even if the payments end up being way more than the contract's actual value. If, however, the policyholder dies an untimely death, depending on the contract type, the insurance company may keep anything left of the money that funded the annuity—nothing would be paid out to the contract holder's survivors. You see where that could make some people balk? Now, modern annuities rarely rely on annuitization for the income portion of the contract, and instead have so many bells and whistles that the old concept of annuitization seems outdated, but because this is still an option, it's important to at least understand the basic concept.

## Riders

Speaking of bells and whistles, let's talk about riders. Modern annuities have a lot of different options these days, many in the form of riders you can add to your contract for a fee—usually about 1 percent of the contract value per year. Each rider has its particulars, and the types of riders available will vary by the type of annuity contract purchased, but I'll just briefly outline some of these little extras:

- Lifetime income rider: Contract guarantees you an enhanced or flexible income for life
- Death benefit rider: Contract pays an enhanced death benefit to your beneficiaries even if you have annuitized
- Return of premium rider: Guarantees you (or your beneficiaries) will at least receive back the premium value of the annuity
- Long-term care rider: Provides a certain amount, sometimes as much as twice the normal income benefit amount for a period of time to help pay for long-term care if the contract holder is moved to a nursing home or assisted living situation

This isn't an extensive look, and usually the riders have fancier names based on the issuing company, like "Lorem Ipsum Insurance Company Income Preferred Bonus Fixed Index Annuity rider," but I just wanted to show you what some of the general options are in layperson's terms.

## Types of Annuities

Annuities break down into four basic types: immediate, variable, fixed, and fixed index.

## Immediate

Immediate annuities primarily rely on annuitization to provide income—you give the insurance company a lump sum up front, and your payments begin immediately. Once you begin receiving income payments, the transaction is irreversible, and you no longer have access to your money in a lump sum. When you die, any remaining contract value is typically forfeited to the insurance company.

All other annuity contract types are "deferred" contracts, meaning you fund your policy as a lump sum or over a period of years and you give it the opportunity to grow over time—sometimes years, sometimes decades.

## Variable

A variable annuity is an insurance contract as well as an investment. It's sold by insurance companies, but only through someone who is registered to sell investment products. With a variable annuity contract, the insurance company invests your premiums in subaccounts that are tied to the stock market. This makes it a bit different from the other annuity contract types because it is the only contract where your money is subject to losses because of market declines. Your contract value has a greater opportunity to grow, but it also stands to lose. Additionally, your contract's value will be subject to the underlying investment's fees and limitations—including income taxes, management fees, etc. Once it is time for you to receive income from the contract, the insurance company will pay you a certain income, locked in at whatever your contract's value was.

## Fixed

A traditional fixed annuity is pretty straightforward. You purchase a contract with a guaranteed interest rate and, when you are ready, the insurance company will make regular income payments to you at whatever payout rate your contract guarantees. Those payments will continue for the rest of your life and, if you choose, for the remainder of your spouse's life.

Fixed annuities don't typically offer significant upside potential, but many people like them for their guarantees (after all, if your Aunt May lives to be ninety-five, knowing she has a paycheck later in life can be her mental and financial safety net), as well as for their predictability. Unlike variable annuities, which are subject to market risk and might be up one year and down the next, you can easily calculate the value of your fixed annuity over your lifetime.

## Fixed Index

To recap, variable annuities take on more risk to offer more possibilities to grow. Fixed annuities have less potential growth, but they protect your principal. In the last couple of decades, many insurance companies have retooled their product line to offer fixed index annuities, which are sort of midway between variable and fixed annuities on that risk/reward spectrum. Fixed index annuities offer greater growth potential than traditional fixed annuities but less than variable annuities. Like traditional fixed annuities, however, fixed index annuities are protected from downside market losses.

Fixed index annuities earn interest that is tied to an external market index, meaning that, instead of your contract value growing at a set interest rate like a traditional fixed annuity, it has the potential to grow within a range. Your contract's value is credited interest based on the performance of an external market index like the S&P 500 while never being invested in the market itself. You can't invest in the S&P 500 directly, but each year, your annuity as the potential to earn interest based on the chosen index's performance, subject to limits set by the company such as caps, spreads and participation rates.

For instance, if your contract caps your interest at 5 percent, then in a year that the S&P 500 gains 3 percent, your annuity value increases 3 percent. If the S&P 500 gains 35 percent, your annuity value gets a 5 percent interest bump. But since your money isn't actually invested in the market with a fixed index annuity, if the market nosedives (such as happened during 2000, 2008 and 2020, anyone?) you won't see any increase in your contract value. Conversely, there will also be no decrease in your contract value—no matter how badly the market performed, as long as you follow the terms of the contract, you won't lose any of the interest you were credited in previous years.

So, what if the S&P 500 shows a market loss of 30 percent? Your contract value isn't going anywhere (unless you purchased an optional rider—this charge will still come out of your annuity value each year). For those more interested in protection than growth potential, fixed index annuities can be an attractive option because, when the stock market has a long period of positive performance, a fixed index annuity can enjoy conservative growth. And, during stretches where the stock market is erratic, and stock values across the board take significant losses? Fixed index annuities won't lose anything due to the stock market volatility.

There is one more way we can use a fixed equity index annuity. We utilize those with no additional income rider. We use it to help protect the principal and lock in any interest credited in previous years. Then, our clients might access the cash value through the penalty-free withdrawal feature (typically, as high as 10 percent of the account value can be accessed without triggering surrender charges) to supplement a family's income.

The withdrawals will be subject to ordinary income taxes and a possible 10 percent federal penalty if they are under fifty-nine-and-one-half, so this strategy is better suited for those nearing or in retirement. This strategy helps us to avoid losses to these funds after years of negative market performance and be a source of income for the following year. It allows us to pull money from a vehicle that did not lose any value due to market loss due to the annuity's principal protection feature.

This can help us to not pull any income from the other funds usually invested in the markets and gives these investments time to potentially recover in the following year.

This strategy intentionally works to help protect this portion of assets from the sequence of returns risk I mentioned earlier in the book. Leave capital that is down in value alone to potentially recover from the markets while accessing capital (in the fixed index annuity) that has been insulated from the market loss—a strategy to consider. Knowing there are strategies that can help counter the sequence of returns risk and enable a higher probability that the nest egg will last a lifetime helps provide confidence.

## Other Things to Know About Annuities

We just talked about the four kinds of annuity contracts available, but all of them have some commonalities as annuities.

For all annuities, the contractual guarantees are only as strong as the insurance company that sells the product, which makes it important to thoroughly check the credit ratings of any company whose products you are considering.

Annuities are tax-deferred, meaning you don't have to pay taxes on interest earnings each year as the contract value grows. Instead, you will pay ordinary income taxes on your withdrawals. These are meant to be long-term products, so, like other tax-deferred or tax-advantaged products, if you begin taking withdrawals from your contract before age fifty-nine-and-one-half, you may also have to pay a 10 percent federal tax penalty. Also, while annuities are generally considered illiquid, some contracts allow you to withdraw up to 10 percent of your contract value every year. Withdraw any more, however, and you could incur additional surrender penalties.

Keep in mind, your withdrawals will deplete the accumulated cash value, death benefit, and, possibly, the rider values of your contract.

We previously discussed why some families are very fortunate to have company pensions. In my career and experience, I have discovered that most families, given a choice, would prefer at least 50 percent of their future income be guaranteed. This is one place where annuities might fit.

In addition to Social Security and corporate pensions, annuities are another efficient source of guaranteed income. As we discussed, there are many kinds of annuity contracts and different designs; some are more appropriate than others, depending on your unique situation.

This is where having a relationship with an experienced financial advisor can come in—Someone that could discuss and explain the different kinds of annuities and the pros and cons of each design that could fit the plan. We believe that our families are smart enough to make great decisions; they just need someone they trust who has no self-serving agenda to help them understand their choices and choose the optimal strategy.

Annuities aren't for everyone, but it's important to understand them before saying "yea" or "nay" on whether they fit into your plan; otherwise, you're not operating with complete information, wouldn't you agree? Regardless, you should talk to a financial professional who can help you understand annuities, help you dissect your particular financial needs, and help show you whether an annuity is appropriate for your retirement income plan.

CHAPTER 8

# Estate & Legacy

In my practice, I devote a significant portion of my time to matters of estates. That doesn't mean drawing up wills or trusts or putting together powers of attorney or anything like that. After all, I'm not an estate planning attorney. But I am a financial professional, and what part of the "estate" isn't affected by money matters?

I've included this chapter because I have seen many people do estate planning wrong. Clients, or clients' families, have come in after experiencing a death in the family and have found themselves in the middle of probate, high taxes, or a discovery of something unforeseen (often long-term care) draining the estate.

I have also seen people do estate planning right: clients or families who visit my office to talk about legacies and how to make them last and adult children who have room to grieve without an added burden of unintended costs, without stress from a family ruptured because of inadequate planning.

I'll share some of these stories here. However, I'm not going to give you specific advice, since everyone's situation is unique. I only want to give you some things to think about and to underscore the importance of planning ahead.

The field of wealth planning is vast. No individual knows everything about this comprehensive discussion, so we like to form strategic partnerships with estate and tax planning attorneys. But not just any attorneys. We love working with those who have a lot of experience and wisdom in family matters to help us with the right estate designs for our families.

The key ingredient is wisdom. That wisdom is often attained by seeing the impact certain design features can have on the next generations. We like to work with attorneys who have worked with the second and third generations and seen the results of the decisions of the first generation.

I have also been fortunate to work with the third and fourth generations of two old money families, as we say. The effect was a mixed result, with more relational devastation than good. I am certain the patriarch of one of the families had different ideas in mind than what played out in his family.

These are the kinds of wisdom I am talking about. Wisdom guides the intention to bless your family and not curse them. Yes, it is possible to curse your family with your wealth. We all know so many examples of it.

So, if you love your family, do something different than just normal traditional planning. Do something unique because your family is unique. We form strategic partnerships with attorneys with wisdom and with unique estate design ideas.

## You Can't Take It With You

When it comes to legacy and estate planning, the most important thing is to *do it*. I have heard people from clients to celebrities (rap artist Snoop Dogg comes to mind) say they aren't interested in what happens to their assets when they die because they'll be dead. That's certainly one way to look at it. But I think that's a very selfish way to go about things—we all have people and causes we care about, and those who care about us. Even if the people we love don't *need* what we leave behind, they can still be fined or legally tied up in the probate process or burial costs if we don't plan for those. And that's not even considering what happens if you become incapacitated at some point while you are still alive. Having a plan in place can greatly reduce the stress of those responsibilities on your loved ones; it's just a loving thing to do.

# Documents

There are a few documents that lay the groundwork of legacy planning. You've probably heard of all or most of them, but I'd like to review what they are and how people commonly use them. These are all things you should talk about with an estate planning attorney to establish your legacy.

## Powers of Attorney

A power of attorney, or POA, is a document giving someone the authority to act on your behalf and in your best interests. These come in handy in situations where you cannot be present (think a vacation where you get stuck in Canada) or, for durable powers of attorney, even when you are incapacitated (think in a coma or coping with dementia).

It is important to have powers of attorney in place and to appoint someone you trust to act on your behalf in these matters. Have you ever heard of someone who was incapacitated after a car accident, whether from head trauma or being in a coma for weeks—sometimes months? Do you think their bills stopped coming due during that time? I like my phone company and my bank, but neither one is about to put a moratorium on sending me bills, particularly not for an extended or interminable period. A power of attorney would have the authority to pay your mortgage or cancel your cable while you are unable.

***You can have multiple POAs
and require them to act jointly.***
What this looks like: Do you think two heads are better than one? One man, Chris, significantly relied on his two sons' opinions for both his business and personal matters. He appointed both sons as joint POA, requiring both their signoffs for his medical and financial matters.

### You can have multiple POAs who can act independently.

What this looks like: Irene had three children with whom she routinely stayed. They lived in different areas of the country, which she thought was an advantage; one month she might be hiking out West, the next she could enjoy the newest off-Broadway production, and the next she could soak up some Southern sun. She named her three children as independently authorized POAs, so, if something happened, no matter where she was, the child closest could step in to act on her behalf.

### You can have POAs who have different responsibilities.

What this looks like: Although Luke's friend Claire, a nurse, was his go-to and POA for health-related issues, financial matters usually made her nervous, so he appointed his good neighbor, Matt, as his POA in all of his financial and legal matters.

In addition to POAs, it may be helpful to have an advanced medical directive. This is a document where you have pre-decided what choices you would make about different health scenarios. An advanced medical directive can help ease the burden for your medical POA and loved ones, particularly when it comes to end-of-life care.

One of the big reasons I became a financial advisor is what happened with my family when my grandmother passed. Her planning was very traditional, not well thought out, and fraught with potential areas of conflict. You see, she survived her husband and had two sons. She made my father (the oldest) the executor of her will. She figured he would know what to do since he was an actuary. My uncle is an accountant and businessman.

My uncle had two sons; the younger son, Werner, was my age. We were like brothers, playing together as kids and going to primary school together until a very sad morning when we received a phone call from my aunt. They were on their way to leave for vacation. While waiting for the rest of the family to finish packing, Werner took his bicycle for a ride. He was in a terrible accident and died three days later from head injuries.

The incident shook our family like no other. I was so young that I did not know what to do with my grief. My strategy was to make his older brother, Heinrich, my hero in life. He was several years older than me, and I certainly was a pest for him as he grew up as a teenager. But all I knew was that I wanted to be around Heinrich as much as possible.

When my grandmother died, my parents, aunt, and uncle started fighting over the heirlooms not described in the will. Also, putting my father in charge of the estate over his younger brother was not at all wise. The net result was that I was not allowed to see Heinrich for three years—although we lived five minutes away from each other—because the adults did not talk to each other. I asked what was going on, but all I could hear from them was that they were fighting over tables, chairs, and dining room sets.

Today, I am passionate about helping my families plan in such a way that their children and grandchildren hug each other six months after they pass away. Why does money have to be so dysfunctionally used by families? Let's change that. Let's plan better to love those we care about and take the time to think out the details. We can help.

The good news is that, after three years, the adults made peace, and we could move on as a family. Today, Heinrich is still a hero to me. He is a professor in emergency medicine in the town in South Africa we grew up in, but I miss my brother, Werner, still today.

## Wills

Perhaps the most basic document of legacy planning, a will is a legal document wherein you outline your wishes for your estate. When it comes to your estate after your death, having a will is the foundation of your legacy. Without one, your loved ones are left behind, guessing what you would have wanted, and the court will likely split your assets according to the state's defaults. Maybe that's exactly what you wanted, as far as anyone knows, right? Because even if you told your nephew he could have your car he's been driving, if it's not in writing, it still might go to the brother, sister, son, or daughter to whom you aren't speaking.

However, it may not be enough just to have a will. Even with a will, your assets will be subject to probate. Probate is what we call the state's process for determining a will's validity. A judge will go through your will to question if it conflicts with state law, if it is the most up-to-date document, if you were mentally competent at the time it was in order, etc. For some, this is a quick, easily-resolved process. For others, particularly if someone steps forward to contest the will, it may take years to settle, all the while subjecting the assets to court costs and attorney's fees.

One other undesirable piece of the probate process is that it is a public process. That means anyone can go to the courthouse, ask for copies of the case, and discover your assets. They can also see who is slated to receive what and who is disputing.

I met, let's call her Edith, through a referral. She was married to, let's call him Bob, and it was her second marriage. During our conversations, I pleaded with her to complete her estate planning. She told me she had a will and already took care of it. In the back of my mind, I felt she had probably done very traditional planning and likely had the minimum needed documents (kind of like my grandmother). So, I kept mentioning it during our monitoring meetings. I also had a sinking feeling that if anything were to happen to her, her children from her first marriage might be at odds with her current husband.

I remember exactly where I was when I got the phone call. It was Bob, and he was crying. He told me that Edith unexpectedly passed away from a cold that turned into an infection.

Two years later, Bob was e sitting in the attorney's office, completing the probate. Her estate had to go through probate because she only had a will. Most people think by having a will, they avoid probate. No, sadly not. You may need a revocable living trust to avoid probate, but I digress. The attorney was discussing the very contentious conversation of the children with Bob, and Bob was worn out completely. They came to a settlement, and the attorney handed his bill for completing the probate. It was over $15,000. Two years, all the emotional stress, and a $15,000 tab at the end—all this could have been avoided if Edith had taken the right steps to help protect her family from this unnecessary strife.

Today I joke that if you do not like your family and love the legal system, please do not do any estate planning. Then, I tell people the story of Edith and Bob.

It's also important to remember beneficiary lines trump wills. So, that large life insurance policy? What if, when you bought it fifteen years ago, you wrote your ex-husband's name on the beneficiary line? Even if you stipulate otherwise in your will, the company that holds your policy will pay out to your ex-spouse. Or, how about the thousands of dollars in your IRA you dedicated to the children thirty years ago, but one of your children was killed in a car accident, leaving his wife and two toddlers behind? That IRA is going to transfer to your remaining children, with nothing for your daughter-in-law and grandchildren.

That may paint a grim portrait, but I can't underscore enough the importance of working with a skilled estate planning attorney to keep your will and beneficiary lines up to date as your life changes.

## Trusts

Another piece of legacy planning to consider is the trust.

A trust is set up through an attorney and allows a third party, or trustee, to hold your assets and determine how they will pass to your beneficiaries. Many people are skeptical of trusts because they assume trusts are only appropriate for the fabulously wealthy.

However, a simple trust will likely cost more than $1,000 if prepared by an attorney and fees can be higher for couples.[49] But a trust can help you avoid both the expense and publicity of probate, provide a more immediate transfer of wealth, avoid some taxes, and provide you greater control over your legacy.

For instance, if you want to set aside some funds for a grandchild's college education, you can make it a requirement he or she enrolls in classes before your trust will dispense any funds. Like a will, beneficiary lines will override your trust conditions, so you must still keep insurance policies and other assets up to date.

Like any financial or legal consideration, there are many options these days beyond the simple "yes or no" question of whether to have a trust. For one thing, you will need to consider if you want your trust to be revocable (you can change the terms while you are alive) or irrevocable (can't be changed; you are no longer the "owner" of the contents). A brief note here about irrevocable trusts: Although they have significant and greater tax benefits, they are still subject to a Medicaid look-back period. This means, if you transfer your assets into an irrevocable trust in an attempt to shelter them from a Medicaid spend-down, you will be ineligible for Medicaid coverage of long-term care for five years. Yet, an irrevocable trust can avoid both probate and estate taxes, and it can even help protect assets from legal judgments against you.

Another thing to remember when it comes to trusts, in general, is, even if you have set up a trust, you must remember to fund it.

I have been in business for more than a quarter-century now, and I love it more today than when I started. What a privilege to be invited into this intimate discussion for a family. It is so exciting to see more dreams come true for our families and to

---

[49] Rickie Houston. smartasset.com. "How Much Does It Cost to Set Up a Trust? https://smartasset.com/estate-planning/how-much-does-it-cost-to-set-up-a-trust

watch the second generation pick up the baton of the first and take it to greater heights.

In my twenty-six years of work, I've had numerous clients come to me, assuming they have helped protect their assets with a trust. When we talk about taxes and other pieces of their legacy, it turns out they never retitled any assets or changed any paperwork on the assets they wanted in the trust. So, please remember, a trust is just a bunch of fancy legal papers if you haven't followed through on retitling your assets.

## Taxes

Although charitable contributions, trusts, and other tax-efficient strategies can reduce your tax bill, it's unlikely your estate will be passed on entirely tax-free. Yet, when it comes to building a legacy that can last for generations, taxes can be one of the heaviest drains on the impact of your hard work.

For 2023, the federal estate exemption was $12.92 million per individual and $25.84 million for a married couple, with estates facing up to a 40 percent tax rate after that. Currently, the new estate limits are set to increase with inflation until January 1, 2026, when they will "sunset" back to the inflation-adjusted 2017 limits.[50] And that's not taking into account the various state regulations and taxes regarding estate and inheritance transfers.

Another tax concern "frequent flyer": retirement accounts.

Your IRA or 401(k) can be a source of tax issues when you pass away. For one thing, taking funds from a sizeable account can trigger a large tax bill. However, if you leave the assets in the account, there are still required minimum distributions (RMDs), which will take effect even after you die. If you pass the account to your spouse, he or she can keep taking your

---

[50] Laura Sanders, Richard Rubin. The Wall Street Journal. March 10, 2022. "Estate and Gift Taxes 2021-2022: "What's New This Year and What You Need to Know." https://www.wsj.com/articles/estate-and-gift-taxes-what-to-know-2021-2022-11646426764

RMDs as is, or your spouse can retitle the account in his or her name and receive RMDs based on his or her life expectancy. Remember, if you don't take your RMDs, the IRS will take up to 25 percent of your required distribution (10 percent if corrections are made in a timely fashion). You will still have to pay income taxes whenever you withdraw that money. Provisions in the original SECURE Act, anyone who inherits your IRA, with few exceptions (your spouse, a beneficiary less than ten years younger, or a disabled adult child, to name a few), will need to empty the account within ten years of your death.

Also—and this is a pretty big also—check with an attorney if you are considering putting your IRA or 401(k) in a trust. An improperly titled beneficiary form for the IRA could mean the difference of thousands of dollars in taxes. This is just one more reason to work with a financial professional, one who can strategically partner with an estate planning attorney to diligently check your decisions.

CHAPTER 9

# Women Retire Too

I help men, women, and families from all walks of life on their journey to and through retirement. Yet, I want to address the female demographic specifically. Why? To be perfectly blunt, women are more likely to deal with poverty than men when they reach retirement. In 2020, the overall poverty rate for women (16.4 percent) exceeded the rate for men (15.7 percent).[51]

The topics, products, and strategies I cover elsewhere in this book are meant to help address retirement concerns for men *and* women, but the dire statistic above is a reminder that much of traditional planning is geared toward men. Male careers, male lifespans, male health care. The bottom line is women's career paths often look much different than men's, so why would their retirement planning look the same?

Women often embrace different roles and values than men as workers, wives, mothers, and daughters. They are more apt to take on roles as caretakers. They often plan for events, worry about loved ones, tend to details, and think about the future. Also, they often want everything to be just right, and they want to be right themselves. It could be you've seen the following affixed to a decorative sign, refrigerator magnet, or T-shirt: "If

---

[51] statistica.com. 2023. "Poverty rate in the United States in 2020, by age and gender" https://www.statista.com/statistics/233154/us-poverty-rate-by-gender/

I agreed with you, we'd both be wrong." The barb features a picture of a woman speaking to a man.

If these characteristics I listed about women are accurate, shouldn't they deserve special considerations from financial professionals? The case can be made, particularly since 69 percent of men in the U.S. age 65 and older happen to be married, compared to 47 percent of women in that age classification.[52] Single women don't have the opportunity to capitalize on the resource pooling and potential economies of scale accompanying a marriage or partnership.

I so strongly believe in this topic that one of the first advisors I hired was a female advisor. Shea understands the financial planning issues for women because she is one. My guidance for women is to work with an experienced female advisor who understands their problems on a more personal level.

We believe so much in this planning that we created a group for our female clients who meet in our "Dream Zone" every quarter. This group is called Women of Wisdom and Wonder. Some of the topics our ladies have discussed include:

- Surviving the death of my spouse
- Caring for my aging parents
- Ways to help my adult children
- Medical and Medicare insurance needs
- Investing 101 and understanding the terms well
- Cybersecurity and ways to help protect yourself
- Taxes and tax planning when you become single
- Ways to understand your monthly statements
- Becoming emotionally and financially prepared for retirement
- And many more

---

[52] Administration for Community Living. November 30, 2022. "Profile of Older Americans." https://acl.gov/aging-and-disability-in-america/data-and-research/profile-older-americans

# Be Informed

It's a familiar scene in many financial offices across the country: A woman comes into an appointment carrying a sack full of unopened envelopes. Often through tears, she sits across the desk from a financial professional and apologizes her way through a conversation about what financial products she owns and where her income is coming from. She is recently widowed and was sure her spouse was taking care of the finances, but now she doesn't know where all their assets are kept, and her confidence in her financial outlook has wavered after walking through funeral expenses and realizing she's down to one income.

Often, she may be financially "okay." Yet, the uncertainty can be wearying, particularly when the family is already reeling from a loss. While this scenario sometimes plays out with men, in my experience, it's more likely to be a woman in that chair across from my desk, probably, in part, because of Western traditions about money management being "a guy thing." But it doesn't have to be this way. This all-too-common scenario can be wiped away with just a little preparation.

## Talk to Your Spouse/
## Work with a Financial Professional

While there are many factors affecting women's financial preparation for and situation in retirement, I cannot emphasize enough that the decision to be informed, to be a part of the conversation, and to be aware of what is going on with your finances is absolutely paramount to a confident retirement. With all the couples I've seen, there is almost always an "alpha" when it comes to finances. It isn't always men—for many of my coupled clients, the wife is the alpha who keeps the books and budgets and knows where all of the family's assets are, down to the penny—yet, statistically, among baby boomers it is usually a man who runs the books. But, as time goes on, it looks like the ratio of male to female financial alphas is evening out. According to a 2019 Gallup study, women are equally as likely to take the lead on finances as men, with 37 percent of U.S. households showing women primarily paying the bills. Half of households also say decisions about savings and investments are shared equally.[53] Whether that's the way your household works or not, there isn't anything wrong with who does what.

The breakdown seems to happen when there is a lack of communication, when no one other than the financial alpha knows how much the family has and where. In the end, it doesn't matter who handles the money; it's about all parties being informed of what's going on financially.

There are a lot of ways to open the conversation about money. One woman started a conversation with her husband, the financial alpha, by sitting down and saying, "Teach me how to be a widow." Perhaps that sounds grim, but it was to the point, and it spurred what she said was a very fruitful conversation. Couples sometimes have their first real conversation about money, assets, and their retirement income approach, in our office. The important thing about having these conversations isn't where, it's when . . . and the best "when" is as soon as possible.

A woman once commented to me that to get this conversation rolling, she asked her husband "to teach her how to be a widow." They spent a day, just one part of an otherwise dull weekend, going through everything she might need to know. They spent the better part of two decades together after that. When he died, and she was widowed, she said the "widowhood" talk had made a huge difference. She knew who to call to talk through their retirement plan and where to call for the insurance policy.

She said the fruit of the weekend exercise they engaged in some twenty years earlier couldn't have been more apparent

---

[53] Megan Brenan. Gallup. January 29, 2020. "Women Still Handle Main Household Tasks in U.S." https://news.gallup.com/poll/283979/women-handle-main-household-tasks.aspx

than when she ultimately accompanied a recently widowed friend of hers to a financial appointment. Her friend was emotional the whole time, afraid she would run out of money any day. The financial professional ultimately showed the friend that she was financially in good shape, but not before the friend had already spent months worried that each check would exhaust her bank account. That's no way to live after losing a loved one. It was preventable had her deceased spouse and financial professional included her in a conversation about "widowhood."

## Spouse-Specific Options

One area where it might be especially important to be on the same page between spouses is when it comes to financial products or services that have spousal options. A few that come to mind are pensions and Social Security, although life insurance and annuity policies also have the potential to affect both spouses.

With pensions, taking the worker's life-only option is somewhat attractive—after all, the monthly payment is bigger. However, you and your spouse should discuss your options. When we're talking about both of you, as opposed to just one lifespan, there is an increased likelihood at least one of you will live a long, long time. This means the monthly payout will be less, but it also ensures that, no matter which spouse outlives the other, no one will have to suffer the loss of a needed pension paycheck in his or her later retirement years.

While we covered Social Security options in a different chapter, I think some of the spousal information bears repeating. Particularly, if you worked exclusively inside the home for a significant number of years, you may want to talk about taking your Social Security benefits based on your spouse's work history. After all, Social Security is based on your thirty-five highest-earning years.

Things to remember about the spousal benefits:[54]
- Your benefit will be calculated as a percentage (up to 50 percent) of your spouse's earned monthly benefit at his or her full retirement age, or FRA.
- For you to begin receiving a spousal benefit, your spouse must have already filed for his or her own benefits and you must be at least sixty-two.
- You can qualify for a full half of your spouse's benefits if you wait until you reach FRA to file.
- Beginning your benefits earlier than your FRA will reduce your monthly check but waiting to file until after FRA will not increase your benefits.

For divorcees:[55]
- You may qualify for an ex-spousal benefit if . . .
    a. You were married for a decade or more
    b. *and* you are at least sixty-two
    c. *and* you have been divorced for at least two years
    d. *and* you are currently unmarried
    e. *and* your ex-spouse is sixty-two (qualifies to begin taking Social Security)
- Your ex-spouse does not need to have filed for you to file on his or her benefit.
- Similar to spousal benefits, you can qualify for up to half of your ex-spouse's benefits if you wait to file until your FRA.
- If your ex-spouse dies, you may file to receive a widow/widower benefit on his or her Social Security record as long as you are at least age sixty and fulfill all the other requirements on the preceding alphabetized list.
    a. This will not affect the benefits of your ex-spouse's current spouse

---

[54] Social Security Administration. "Retirement Planner: Benefits For You As A Spouse." https://www.ssa.gov/planners/retire/applying6.html
[55] Social Security Administration. "Retirement Planner: If You Are Divorced." https://www.ssa.gov/planners/retire/divspouse.html

For widow's (or widower's, for that matter) benefits:[56]
- You may qualify to receive as much as your deceased spouse would have received if . . .
    a. You were married for at least nine months before his or her death
    b. *or* you would qualify for a divorced spousal benefit
    c. *and* you are at least sixty
    d. *and* you did not/have not remarried before age sixty
- You may earn delayed credits on your spouse's benefit *if* your spouse hadn't already filed for benefits when he or she died.
- Other rules may apply to you if you are disabled or are caring for a deceased spouse's dependent or disabled child.

# Longevity

On average, women live longer than men. Most stats put average female longevity at about two years more than men. But averages are tricky things. An April 2022 report by the World Economic Forum listed the eight oldest people in the world to all be women. They ranged in age from 118 years old to 114 and included two Americans.[57]

On one hand, this is a Brandi Chastain moment. You know, when the American soccer icon shed her jersey to celebrate a game-winning penalty kick to win the World Cup. Seriously, how fabulous are women? They tend to be meticulous, resolute,

---

[56] Social Security Administration. "Survivors Planner: If You Are The Worker's Widow Or Widower."
https://www.ssa.gov/planners/survivors/ifyou.html#h2
[57] Martin Armstrong. World Economic Forum. April 29, 2022. "How old are the world's oldest people?" https://www.weforum.org/agenda/2022/04/the-oldest-people-in-the-world/

perseverant. On the other hand, the trend for women to live longer presents longstanding financial ramifications. We count it an honor to work with widows. Most of the time, we work with them because our wives tend to outlive us. In fact, the average life expectancy favors women to outlive men by five years.[58]

## Simply Needing More Money in Retirement

Living longer in retirement means needing more money, period. Barring a huge lottery win or some crazy stock market action, the date you retire is likely the point at which you have the most money you will ever have. Not to put too grim a spin on it, but the problem with longevity is, the further you get away from that date, the further your dollars have to stretch. If you planned to live to a nice eighty-something but live to a nice one-hundred-something, that is *two decades* you will need to account for, monetarily.

To put this in perspective, let's say you like to drink coffee as an everyday splurge. Not accounting for inflation or leap years, a $2.50 cup-a-day habit is $18,250 over a two-decade span. Now, think of all the things you like to do that cost money. Add those up for twenty years of unanticipated costs. I think you'll see what I mean.

During the 2020 onset of the coronavirus pandemic, many learned to cut costs. For some, that amounted to skipping their decadent latte. For others, however, cutbacks became acute. According to data compiled by Age Wave and Edward Jones, 32 percent of Americans plan to retire later than planned because of the pandemic. Women felt a more adverse effect. The report stipulated that 41 percent of women continued to save for retirement, compared to 58 percent of men.[59]

---

[58] Tyler Santora. livescience.com. July 11, 2021. "Why do women tend to outlive men?" https://www.livescience.com/why-women-outlive-men.html
[59] Megan Leonhardt. cnbc.com. June 16, 2021. "58% of men were able to continue saving for retirement during the pandemic—but only 41% of women were." https://www.cnbc.com/2021/06/16/why-pandemic-hit-womens-retirement-savings-more-than-mens.html

## More Health Care Needs

In addition to the cost of living for a longer lifespan is the fact aging, plain and simple, means more health care, and more health care means more money. Women are survivors. They suffer from the morbidity-mortality paradox, which states women suffer more non-fatal illnesses throughout their lifetime than men, who experience fewer illnesses but higher mortality.

Women have been found to seek treatment more often when not feeling well and emphasize staying healthy when older, according to studies.[60] So survival is on the side of the woman. However, surviving things, like cancer, also means more checkups later in life.

A statistical concern for women involves the prospect of long-term care. Long-term care for women lasts 3.7 years on average compared to 2.2 years for men.[61]

## Widowhood

Not only do women typically live longer than their same-age male counterparts, they also stand a greater chance of living alone as they age. Some divorce, separate or never marry. Among those age sixty-five and over, 33 percent of women live alone compared to 20 percent of men.[62]

I don't write this to scare people; rather, I think it's fundamentally important to prepare my female clients for

---

[60] advisory.com. July 22, 2020. "Why do women live longer than men? It's more complicated than you think." https://www.advisory.com/en/daily-briefing/2020/07/22/longevity
[61] Lindsay Modglin. singlecare.com. February 15, 2022. "Long-term care statistics 2022" https://www.singlecare.com/blog/news/long-term-care-statistics/
[62] statistica.com. November 23, 2022. "Share of senior households living alone in the United States 2020, by gender" https://www.statista.com/statistics/912400/senior-households-living-alone-usa/

something that may be a startling, *but very likely*, scenario. At some point, most women will have to handle their financial situations on their own. A little preparation can go a long way, and having a basic understanding of your household finances and the "who, what, where, and how much" of your family's assets is incredibly useful—it can prevent a tragic situation from being more traumatic.

In my opinion, the financial services industry sometimes underserves women in these situations. Some financial professionals tend to alienate women, even when their spouses are alive. I've heard several stories of women who sat through meeting after meeting without their financial professional ever addressing a single question to them.

In our firm, when we work with couples, we work hard to make sure our retirement income strategies work for *both* people. No matter who the financial alpha is, it's important for everyone affected by a retirement strategy to understand it.

I remember a year that was difficult for two of our families. They each lost a husband, father, and friend. Both deaths were sudden and unexpected.

In putting the pieces back together, we had to come alongside one widow and help her sell her husband's business. The sad reality is that the business was sold at 50 percent of the price per valuation just a year before because the husband did not conduct adequate succession planning.

We help a widow through the tedious process of consolidating accounts in her name, filing all the forms for life insurance proceeds, and getting title and registration of all assets in her name. We work with the family's estate planning attorney if any assets need to go through probate. Even though we plan to avoid it, there might be small accounts only in his name that might have to go through probate.

We help rebuild the retirement income plan for one spouse and reassess the investment strategy for an immediate retirement scenario. It is like we are going through our whole planning process again, but this time for just the surviving spouse. We end our planning by reassessing, working with experienced estate planning attorneys, what her estate plan should look like now that she is single. We value working with the entire family, especially the children, so they also can see and understand that their mother is financially healthy.

One blessing that occurred this year is that one of our widows spoke at the WOW event for our lady clients, explaining all the little details we had to deal with. For instance, do you and your spouse know each other's passwords to websites, cellphones, computers, etc.? Through better planning, these obstacles can be avoided. She blessed our ladies with insights from her experience.

These are very somber times, and we are trying to make it a little better by helping our newly widowed clients as much as we can. We are helping them to rebuild for what lies ahead. One final experience that has been very rewarding for me was going to a car dealer with one of our widows who lost her husband three years ago. Just to be with her and help her think through everything a single woman has to think about in choosing a car.

## Taxes

One of the often-unexpected aspects of widowhood is the tax bill. Many women continue similar lifestyles to the ones they shared with their spouses. This, in turn, means continuing to have a similar need for income. However, after the death of a spouse, their taxes will be calculated based on a single filer's income table, which is much less forgiving than the couple's tax rates. With proper planning, your financial professional and tax advisor may be able to help you take the sting out of your new tax status.

## Caregiving

Caregiving.org updates its national report about every five years. According to its findings released in 2020, of the 53 million caregivers providing unpaid, informal care for older adults, 61 percent are women. Among today's family caregivers, 61 percent work and 45 percent report some kind of financial impact from providing a loved one care and support.[63]

In addition to the financial burden created by caregiving responsibilities, women often devote many hours each day to duties such as housekeeping and looking after loved ones. So then, when can women find the time to focus long and hard on financial matters?

Unfortunately, the impact and hardships created by traditional roles for women typically do not account for Social Security benefit losses or the losses of health care benefits and retirement savings. This also doesn't account for maternity care, mothers who homeschool, or women who leave the workforce to care for their children in any way.

I don't repeat these statistics to scare you. Not only are unpaid family caregivers spending their time and energy taking care of others, but they're also putting their own money towards the cause. An AARP study found that three-quarters of family caregivers surveyed were spending an average of $7,242 a year on out-of-pocket caregiving costs.[64]

Yet, I think the emotional value of the care many women provide their elderly relatives or neighbors cannot be quantified. So, to be clear, this shouldn't be taken as a "why not to provide caregiving" spiel. Instead, it should be seen as a call for "why to *prepare* for caregiving" or "how to lessen the financial and emotional burden of caregiving."

## Funding Your Own Retirement

For these reasons, women should be prepared to fund more of their own retirements. There are several savings options and

---

[63] caregiving.org. 2020 Report. "Caregiving in the U.S. 2020." https://www.caregiving.org/caregiving-in-the-us-2020/

[64] Nancy Kerr. AARP. June 29, 2021. " Family Caregivers Spend More Than $7,200 a Year on Out-of-Pocket Costs." https://www.aarp.org/caregiving/financial-legal/info-2021/high-out-of-pocket-costs.html

products, including the spousal 401(k). Unlike a traditional 401(k), where you contribute money to a plan with your employer, a spousal 401(k) is something your spouse sets up on your behalf, so he or she can contribute a portion of the paycheck to your retirement funds. This is something to consider, particularly for families where one spouse has dropped out of the workforce to care for a relative.

Also, if you find yourself in a caregiving role, talk to your employer's human resources department. Some companies have paid leave, special circumstance, or sick leave options you could qualify for, making it easier to cope and helping you stay in the workforce longer.

## Saving Money

Women likely need more money to fund their retirements, period. But this doesn't have to be a significant burden—often, women are better at saving, while usually taking less risk in their portfolios.[65] This gives me reason to believe, as women get more involved in their finances, families will continue to be more confident for retirement, both *his* and *hers*.

---

[65] Maurie Backman. The Motley Fool. March 4, 2021. "A Summary of 20 Years of Research and Statistics on Women in Investing." https://www.fool.com/research/women-in-investing-research/

CHAPTER 10
# Charity

Wills and testaments, trusts and powers of attorney—these are all pieces of what we often call legacy planning. But I would be remiss if I didn't address a piece of legacy preparation near and dear to my heart: charitable contributions.

Charity is one of those universal concepts that unites us as human beings. Football players who dedicate their resources to building homes for single moms, communities who help neighbors rebuild after catastrophes, groundskeepers who donate millions from under a mattress to their favorite university, or private donors who put impoverished children through school . . . these are the stories that inspire us, that drive us to be better people.

There are many, many ways to pass money to your favorite charity, university, foundation, or public resource. Some include using qualified charitable distributions with the mandatory withdrawals from your IRA, and others lend themselves to establishing trusts. Whatever your preferred method of charitable distribution, the right financial professional will partner with a qualified tax advisor and/or estate planning attorney to discover how to help you make your contributions in a way that fits well within your own strategy for taxes—helping to ensure your contributions are passed efficiently to your intended beneficiary.

I grew up in South Africa, the country with the largest disparity in income between the haves and have-nots. There is an economic index to measure this called the Gini index.[66] Also, unemployment in South Africa has been above 25 percent for quite some time.[67] With those pieces of context, you might understand the following.

Every day the front doorbell rang, and it was either an individual or a couple asking for a job, something to eat, clothes, or even if they could use our garden hose for a sip of water. So, it is fair to say I grew up with a strong responsibility to use the gifts I have received—a loving family, a safe home, and an excellent education—to work with those in need and become very productive in society. I was determined to make a living for myself and my family and have enough to help the hurting world around me. In South Africa, the needs are staring you in the face every day. At times, it is more difficult to see in America, but it is still there.

In the rest of the world, we see desperate need everywhere, and lately, we see the needs of the Ukrainians in the war against Russia.

I believe there is no higher honor than to use the gifts the good Lord gave all of us and apply them to make this a better place to live for everyone. I also believe in helping those who are motivated to improve their situation.

The joy of giving is intoxicatingly good and gives us so much fulfillment.

## Where to Start?

We've all heard it is better to give than to receive, and science backs this up. Multiple studies show those who give to charity

---

[66] The World Bank. "Gini index" https://data.worldbank.org/indicator/SI.POV.GINI?most_recent_value_desc=true

[67] macrotrends.net. "South Africa Unemployment Rate 1991-2022" https://www.macrotrends.net/countries/ZAF/south-africa/unemployment-rate

or volunteer experience less depression, lower blood pressure, higher self-esteem, and greater happiness.[68]

It's a common perception, however, that retirees are less inclined to be charitable. It seems like reasoned logic—they're living on fixed incomes, and it's difficult to work charitable giving into conservative strategies designed to protect assets. But this counters the facts. In 2021, more baby boomers donated to charities than any other generations.[69]

So, how do we keep up—or even increase—our donations in retirement? Well, as with all the other topics we cover in this book, step one is to build charitable giving into our retirement plans. Advanced planning can help you be sure your donations—at least in the monetary sense—are given in the most tax-efficient and effective way, both for you and for the charity to which you are contributing.

## Planned Giving: Lifetime

When we're talking about charitable contributions, it's important to distinguish between lifetime giving and charitable giving as part of a well-prepared estate plan.

The American tax system has many provisions to encourage charitable giving. I'm sure the reasoning goes something along the lines of, if we the people were naturally able, through our own means, to care for the poor and vulnerable in our own communities, we collectively would need to pay fewer taxes to support federal aid to those same people. It's a wonderful consideration, and one we should all aspire to. But, in practice, it gets more difficult, as tax codes change and shift according to

---

[68] "Volunteering and Its Surprising Benefits."
https://www.helpguide.org/articles/healthy-living/volunteering-and-its-surprising-benefits.htm
[69] Dawn Papandrea. Lendingtree. November 29, 2021. "56% of Americans Donated to Charity in 2021, at Average of $574."
https://www.lendingtree.com/debt-consolidation/charitable-donations-survey-study/

political administrations and other public considerations. Ensuring your charitable contributions are tax-efficient is not a one-time move—it requires yearly analysis.

It's important to remember your charitable giving is most effective when the combined amount of your *itemized* deductions is more than your *standard* deduction. Now it isn't only charity that counts toward your itemized deduction; there are also homeowner and business owner credits, adoption credits, etc. But, as it pertains to charity, if you haven't contributed a significant amount to charity in a certain tax year, it may not be worth counting on your taxes.

Deductions change year-to-year, of course, but the IRS usually publishes the following year's charts in November. When you're itemizing deductions, you may deduct up to 50 percent of your adjusted gross (pre-tax) income, though in some cases, 20 percent and 30 percent limitations apply.[70]

Another thing to keep in mind if you are considering the tax implications of a charitable donation, you must have a receipt, a canceled check, or some demonstrable way of recording the transaction. Additionally, many charitable activities aren't eligible for tax credits. Raffle tickets, charity event entrance fees, and those sorts of things are not typically counted as charitable deductions on your taxes—a quick rule of thumb is, if you received something in return for your donation, it's not tax-deductible.

Perhaps one of the most crucial things to keep in mind when it comes to the tax implications of charitable giving, however, is "nonprofit" doesn't mean "tax-advantaged." The IRS keeps a long list of organizations that qualify for tax-deducted gifting in the Internal Revenue Code section 501(c)(3). Yet, many excellent nonprofits and civic organizations are not 501(c)(3)s. That doesn't mean you shouldn't give to them—truly, charity is *not* about tax deductions when it comes right down to it—it just

---

[70] IRS.gov. August 25, 2022. "Charitable Contribution Deductions" https://www.irs.gov/charities-non-profits/charitable-organizations/charitable-contribution-deductions#.

means you shouldn't plan to include it as part of your tax-efficiency strategies.

Again, I would be remiss to not emphasize that these laws and definitions change year to year, so it is important to work with a team of qualified financial and tax professionals who can help you plan for the future and adjust to the times, in addition to verifying whether the charity you are considering is tax-exempt.

While impermanence seems to be a fixture of our tax system, one important aspect of charity tax law was made permanent for the foreseeable future. In 2015, Congress passed a budget deal signed into law by President Barack Obama. Among the provisions of the "Protecting Americans From Tax Hikes Act of 2015," which included this important measure::

> IRA charitable rollovers — at age seventy-two, owners of traditional IRAs can make direct gifts of up to $100,000 a year to a qualified charity directly from the IRA.[71] This is known as a qualified charitable distribution, or QCD.

What makes permanent deduction No. 3 so important is a person who uses an IRA to contribute to charity in this way can: 1. Be charitable, 2. Avoid having their RMDs push them into a higher tax bracket by instead gifting them to those in need, 3. Take advantage of the tax-free aspect of a QCD when planning charitable gifting, and 4. Potentially use the tax break to offset other tax consequences, like the tax on appreciated assets or capital gains. Please note, though, since the SECURE Act allows IRA contributions after an individual reaches age seventy-two, QCDs will be adversely affected (not all of the listed benefits will still apply) if a contribution is made to that IRA in the same year a QCD is withdrawn.[72]

---

[71] Council on Foundations. 2022. "IRA Charitable Rollover" https://www.cof.org/content/ira-charitable-rollover-0#:~:text=As%20of%20December%2018%2C%202015,recognize%20the%20distribution%20as%20income.

[72] Bob Carlson. Forbes. January 28,2020. "More Questions and Answers About the SECURE Act."

The families we work with also like to give and make a difference. We often use the tool of a donor-advised fund to help our families create a family-giving account. This tool can often be efficient for estate planning as well. The donor-advised fund becomes the family's giving account and allows the heirs to participate. Helping families decide whether to pay taxes or create family impact dollars gives us great joy.

The United States tax code allows families to send money to their communities rather than send it to Washington, DC. When we ask most families what they prefer, most select to help their communities in the areas of passion they have. Unfortunately, it is not a dollar-for-dollar benefit, but it nevertheless can help provide tax relief. What is exciting about using a donor-advised fund is that the family now has a giving account and can start formulating the family-giving statement.

Here, we make additional decisions about how much, where, when, how, and what to give. After a family wrestles with these questions, they are able to optimize the joy from community giving. I often see how they do this with their children and enjoy impact and fun while experiencing a higher level of fulfillment together.

## Planned Giving: After My Lifetime

For many charities, endowments and legacy gifts are the lifeblood that keeps them going. And, for many of us, a large final gift is an excellent way to continue a legacy of giving into perpetuity. The financial reasons for final charitable gifts, much like the annual contributions we often give, are many and, mostly, tax-based. A large final gift can be a good way to offload highly appreciated assets, allowing our favorite charities to experience the full use of an asset without us having to pay out a sizable tax bill.

---

https://www.forbes.com/sites/bobcarlson/2020/01/28/more-questions-and-answers-about-the-secure-act/#113d49564869

Many charities have gone to great lengths to make this an attractive option, with some having preferences for certain donation types and strategies. For instance, many public entities, such as libraries and schools, have foundations to collect most of the donations and do major fundraising. Churches and universities often have special projects and intentional funding that stems from sizable endowments.

There are many financial vehicles to help you meet your charitable goals and give you benefits during your lifetime as well—from permanent life insurance policies to charitable trusts and charitable annuities. That's why it's important to plan ahead and work with a goal in mind. If you have some idea of what end you want to achieve, it can be easier to find the estate attorneys, tax professionals, and financial professionals who will be best qualified to help.

# Non-Monetary Charitable Contributions

Ultimately, aside from the tax breaks, the good feeling, and the name on a park bench you might receive, your charitable contributions aren't about what you "get" in return. This is one other reason we should plan ahead for our good works; it's about doing the right thing.

Volunteering is one great, non-monetary way to support the charities and causes we believe in. Like I noted earlier, research shows retirees who are active and engaged volunteers in their communities often have a better sense of purpose and report more happiness than those who aren't. In volunteering, we have a reason to get up in the morning, and we meet new people and make friends. These are all things that may previously have stemmed from your nine-to-five workday but tend to fall by the wayside after leaving the workforce, making this consideration even more important.

At The LifeWealth Group, we conduct volunteer days with all our clients and family members. Whoever wants to join us comes together for an afternoon or sometimes a whole day. We work together at a food bank or support a Christmas toy drive or a Saturday event for the families of children with disabilities.

We also love to support the nonprofit organizations that our families work with. In addition, we invite our clients to galas and fundraising events for charities we know they are passionate about. We all learn about new charities together, and we enjoy serving together.

My team enjoys interacting with our clients, and often our clients invite their friends. It is much more fun to serve a charity in a group setting.

So, this is how we are having fun and igniting the families we serve to get involved in their communities. Our families are one way we leave a legacy. But charitable giving—with our time, our talents, and our treasure—allows us to extend our legacies even further, beyond passing on Grandpa's nose or Grandma's ticklish feet.

CHAPTER 11

# Finding a Financial Professional

I grew up during a period in South Africa comparable to the Great Depression in the US. When walking down the street, if my siblings or I spotted a bolt, nail, or nut, we picked it up and placed it in a glass jar in the garage to use later. We would cut a two-liter plastic soda container in half and use half as a container and the other half as a funnel. We would reuse or repurpose many possessions. We grew up with a mindset that dictated we optimize or maximize our limited resources.

While I have found America to be an incredible land abundant in resources, I want our clients to make the most of the resources they have to fulfill their dreams and perhaps even ignite more ambitions. The first step is to help clients through our LifeWealth Dream Builder process, which we implement to develop their plan. Our approach helps clients focus on the vision they have for their wealth, the wealth of their family, and the wealth of their community.

Sometimes, it feels like I have to give people permission to dream again. They become so focused on work-related matters that it can be easy to forget the end goal they're working toward. Rediscovering their dream for life and vision for their future often inspires them into a joyous thought process, and their dreams become visible.

We believe everyone needs someone skillful enough to ask the right questions and help develop the right sequence of steps to build into a written retirement plan. The vision resides within all of us, but it can be advantageous to connect with someone—financial professionals in our case—to extract the dreams and ambitions we each covet.

At first, the process can seem a bit whimsical, especially to someone focused on the numbers reflected by their assets. I remember a CPA I worked with who was pretty straightforward and taciturn. He flashed a wry smile when I began talking about dreams and ambitions for him and his spouse, then asked if we could just get down to the numbers.

Still, he humored me. He took home the empty dream list we gave him with the instructions, "Ask your wife what she dreams about accomplishing." Together, he and his wife filled out the dream list.

Later, after becoming a client, he introduced me to the Board of Directors for a nonprofit organization I eventually helped with some matters. He shared with the Board the dream list I asked him and his wife to complete and admitted he laughed it off. But as he continued, he told of a vacation trip he and his wife had just taken to visit Israel. He conceded that the destination had never been on his radar, but his wife longed to see the Holy Land. He found the sites amazing and commented on his wife's excitement.

The revelations of this client reinforced my belief in the beauty of seeing our dreams come true.

Those dreams frequently do not correspond with a financial statement measured in dollars. People, even highly successful people, are looking for something beyond their earnings and their experiences. They're often looking for a level of fulfillment they cannot get from money. We work with many wealthy people. We find that they like us to help them surrender some of their devotion to building wealth to gain additional satisfaction in their lives.

I consider one international phenomenon connected to generational wealth a pet peeve. Although different cultures express it differently, I call it going from "shirt sleeves to shirt sleeves in three generations." The concept is that the first generation creates wealth, the second generation keeps the wealth out of fear of losing it, and the third generation indeed spends all the wealth.

What a tragedy, from poverty to wealth and back to poverty. Yet wealth can destroy families. I am highly motivated to change that phenomenon within my own family and the families with whom we work. The mission demands intention.

At The LifeWealth Group, we record dreams during conversations with clients. We write them down and have clients do so, too. We quantify those dreams. Then we incorporate them into each client's retirement plan.

When those dreams come to fruition, we encourage clients to snap pictures. At our office, those photos adorn our "Dream Wall," an inspirational collection depicting clients who lived out their dreams. Our team loves that we celebrate right alongside clients by helping them plan out each step of the journey.

Our collection of keepsakes on that wall continues to grow. We're privileged to post those photos. Through the growth of our company, I have had opportunities to meet and be around many famous people. I consider that journey quite eventful, considering I didn't recognize the famous faces on US currency when Janice and I began building our future in Florida.

But I refrain from hanging pictures of me alongside famous people. Our clients are our heroes. They engage in what can become the most rewarding journeys of their lives by fulfilling their dreams. We play a role in their accomplishments by helping them discover what they truly value from life and recognizing that is what retirement is about. Still, our Dream Wall is a fitting tribute to those who motivate us to continue and improve the work we do at The LifeWealth Group.

If we could pinpoint a single goal for our company, it would be to see more dreams come true for you, your family, and your most passionate causes and charities. We take a unique, independent approach to building a plan that helps you find more confidence, freedom, joy, happiness, and impact. We call that the abundant life for generations.

## Fees

In recent years, advertising in your local newspaper has diminished. So too has the size of the paper. More people are accustomed to reading news online, or look for other sources, including those without a paywall. Advertisers don't find as much value in placing ads in the actual print version of the paper. Declines in circulation are primarily to blame. Also, many former advertisers have company websites, which they use to drive consumer traffic.

However, if you happen to be someone who receives the newspaper in your driveway, you might have noticed that grocery store circulars are still a thing. Sure, the circulars might be a bit smaller. Yet, grocers still see some advantages to listing numerous prices for sales items in print, which readers can often scan much easier than looking up individual items on a website.

Those newspaper ads continue to be printed as a service to consumers. They want to see prices—in some cases before they ever step into the store—so they can prepare their shopping lists accordingly.

Why then should the cost of doing business with a financial professional often seem like a clandestine mystery? Well, to be blunt, it shouldn't. Consumers should know how much it will cost them to work with a financial professional and how exactly they arrive at the fees charged.

Now, fees can be troublesome. You can't get something for nothing, and fees are how many financial companies and professionals make a living. Yet, it's important to recognize even a fee of a single percentage point is money out of your pocket—money that represents not just the one-time fee of today but also represents an opportunity cost. For someone approaching retirement, how much do you think fees may have cost them over their lifetime?

It is important to look at management fees and assess if you think you're getting what you pay for.

# Acknowledgments

I have several mentors who have been very instrumental in my career and my personal development.

I want to thank Tom Goldman, who bought an advertisement from me and "reverse sold" me on becoming a financial advisor at Equitable. Tom, thank you for your mentorship and all the fun meetings we enjoyed in the first year of my career. Many of the phrases I use in conversation today stem from the lessons I learned from you.

Thank you to John van der Wiede, my first boss and mentor when I joined Equitable. John, you really cared about your agents. You taught us the technical aspects of the business and how to market with excellence. But what I cherish the most is our friendship and the time we worked together again when you joined my firm. You are a great friend, and I always enjoy our golf outings and conversation.

To Bobb Biehl, a life and business mentor: I believe you are the wisest man this side of heaven. Through our conversations, the books you wrote, and the tools you developed, you taught me how to help my clients in wise and practical ways.

I also want to thank Don Blanton, whose tools helped me learn and handle complex client issues. You have also helped me tremendously in my personal journey. You have been a great inspiration to me to be the best leader and person I can be.

Finally, I want to thank Hilton, my oldest son, who spent time with me, helping me write this book. English is my second language but luckily, Hilton's first language. To see you love this business and help our families is a delight and makes me very proud of you. You have a love for people and many great talents to help people for many years to come.

# *About the Author*

**HILGARDT LAMPRECHT, CFP®, CKA®, CExP™**
**The LifeWealth Group**

As the CEO and Financial Advisor of The LifeWealth Group, Hilgardt creates holistic financial plans customized to each client's personal and financial goals. Plans are designed to help maximize their LifeWealth, instill confidence as they approach retirement, and empower them to feel like they are a part of something impactful for generations to come. "LifeWealth" is about more than money.

Hilgardt got his start in the industry in 1997 as an agent at Equitable, a financial services company in Orlando, Florida. Five years later, he became an independent financial advisor. At the time this book was published, The LifeWealth Group just celebrated its twentieth anniversary in business.

Many have called The story of the journey that led the company to where it is now inspirational. After growing up in South Africa, Hilgardt uses his academic and life experiences to help the families he serves to shape their futures. He journeys alongside those families to help them accomplish their dreams. Hilgardt truly enjoys working with high-capacity, high-impact families to fuel more dreams, resulting in more adventure and life impact.

Hilgardt holds insurance licenses in Florida, Alabama, Alaska, Arizona, California, Washington DC, Georgia, Illinois, Massachusetts, Maryland, Michigan, Missouri, Mississippi, Montana, North Carolina, New Hampshire, Nevada, Ohio, South Carolina, South Dakota, Texas, Virginia, and Wisconsin. His state insurance license numbers are OE56515 in California and 1237880 in Texas. He has earned his CERTIFIED FINANCIAL PLANNER™ (CFP®), Certified Kingdom Advisor (CKA®), and Certified Exit Planner (CExP™) designations.

Hilgardt has a Bachelor of Accountancy from the University of Stellenbosch in South Africa, and an Honors Bachelor of Accounting Science from the University of South Africa. He holds his Florida health, life, and variable annuity insurance license and has passed the Series 6, 7, 24, 63, and 65 securities exams.

Hilgardt has been published or quoted in Kiplinger, Nasdaq, Finupance.com, Tribunecontentagency.com, AE Insider, and Winter Garden City Lifestyle and Stroll Oakland Park magazines.

Hilgardt and Janice have been married for twenty-eight years and have three sons and a new puppy. Their oldest son, Hilton, joined the practice in 2020 and currently serves as an advisor. As a family man, Hilgardt naturally has a passion and need to see those in his family feel uplifted, inspired, and living an abundant life. This passion overflows to his extended "LifeWealth Family," which includes his team and clients and is evident in his decisions and how he relates to each individual.

Hilgardt is an avid reader and is continuously seeking personal and professional growth. Hilgardt enjoys golfing and spending time with family and friends in his spare time.

**WINTER GARDEN**
270 W. Plant Street, Suite 240
Winter Garden, Florida 34787

**Phone:** 407.2994129
**Email:** youradvisor@lifewealthgroup.com
**Web:** thelifewealthgroup.com

Made in the USA
Middletown, DE
25 March 2025

73258264R00085